D0501091

The Book of
PAPER
CUTTING

The Book of PAPER CUTTING

A Complete Guide to All the Techniques—With More Than 100 Project Ideas

CHRIS RICH

Sweetheart Tree, *J. de Jong-Brouwer*

A Sterling/Lark Book
Sterling Publishing Co., Inc.   New York

Art Director: Chris Colando
Production: Elaine Thompson, Chris Colando, Charlie Covington
Translation: Charlotte Smith

Library of Congress Cataloging-in-Publication Data

Rich, Chris, 1949–
    The book of paper cutting : a complete guide to all the techniques with more than 100 project ideas / by Chris Rich.
       p.   cm.
    "A Sterling/Lark book."
    Includes bibliographical references and index.
    ISBN 0-8069-0285-X : $21.95
    1. Paper work. I. Title
TT870.R468   1993
736'.98--dc20   92-21536
                                     CIP

10 9 8 7 6 5 4 3 2

A Sterling/Lark Book

Produced by Altamont Press, Inc.
50 College St., Asheville, NC 28801

Published in 1993 by Sterling Publishing Co., Inc.
387 Park Ave. S., New York, NY 10016

© 1993 Altamont Press

Portions of this book have been published previously in *Leer Knippende Zien*, by I. G. Kerp-Schlesinger. Uitgeverij Canticleer bv, de Bilt, Holland, © 1970. Acknowledgements for photographs reprinted from this book can be found on page 126.

Distributed in Canada by Sterling Publishing,
   c/o Canadian Manda Group, P.O. Box 920, Station U, Toronto,
   Ontario M8Z 5P9
Distributed in the United Kingdom by Cassell PLC, Villiers House,
   41/47 Strand, London WC2N 5JE, England
Distributed in Australia by Capricorn Link, Ltd., P.O. Box 665,
   Lane Cove, NSW 2066

The artists contributing to *The Book of Papermaking* retain copyrights on their individual works presented in this volume.

Every effort has been made to ensure that all information in this book is accurate. However, due to differing conditions, tools, and individual skills, the publisher cannot be responsible for any injuries, losses, or other damages which may result from the use of the information in this book.

All rights reserved.

Printed in Hong Kong.

ISBN 0-8069-0285-X

TABLE OF CONTENTS

INTRODUCTION

Cutting techniques differ from country to country. The flowers were cut, in traditional Chinese fashion, with a craft knife on a single sheet of flat rice paper. The heart design was cut with scissors from a piece of single-folded paper, in the style of German and Swiss scherenschnitte artists and the Polish rooster wycinanka was constructed by layering cut pieces of paper.

TOP LEFT Rooster,
    13" (33 cm) x 13" (33 cm),
    © 1989, Elzbieta Kaleta

TOP RIGHT Flowers,
    11" (27.9 cm) x 14" (35.6 cm),
    Alex Fong

OPPOSITE Peaceful Glen,
    7" (17.8 cm) x 9" (22.9 cm),
    © 1983, Marie-Helene Grabman

Papercutting—what is it? The answers always vary: craft and folk art, pastime and vocation, an evening's fun and a life's work. Papercutting is design and symmetry. It's collage. It's decorative or functional or both. It's silhouettes and stencils, Polish roosters and Pennsylvania German valentines, framed art, ornaments, and more. Papercutting—in all its various forms—is an ancient art, a gentle teacher, and a constant pleasure.

Although its popularity has waxed and waned, cut paper has fascinated people for nearly two thousand years. Millions of men and women—from China to Germany and Holland to Japan—have snipped, incised, sliced, punched, and carved their unique, paper visions of the world. Today, papercutting is experiencing a resurgence, perhaps because it offers so many rewards while making so few demands.

Papercutting welcomes beginners and experts alike. If you're a novice, you'll be relieved to know that the basic skills are easy to learn, and the required tools are few: scissors, knives, perhaps a pencil or two, and steady hands. A child can cut a simple pattern in under fifteen minutes, but the artist who seeks challenges will find that papercutting offers many. Some sophisticated patterns take astounding ingenuity and skill to design and cut. In fact, a single work can require weeks or even months—and thousands of snips or slices—to complete.

This book will introduce you to both the act and the art of cutting paper. In it you'll find everything you need except the tools themselves: a bit of history, complete instructions for the novice papercutter, some of today's finest designs, and a wide range of projects to suit every taste and skill level. Whether you're an accomplished cutter in search of new ideas or someone entirely new to papercutting's possibilities, inspiration awaits you within these pages.

PAPERCUTTING AROUND THE WORLD

papercutting	English
scherenschnitte (sher-en-**shnit**-uh)	German and Swiss
wycinanki (vee-chee-**non**-kee)	Polish
monkiri (mon-kee-ree)	Japanese
chien-chih (**jian**-jeh)	Chinese (paper cutting)
k'e-chih (**kuh**-jeh)	Chinese (paper carving)
knippen (**knip**-pen)	Dutch

PAPERCUTTING:

A BRIEF HISTORY

The history of papercutting is as complex and fragile as the most finely cut wycinanki or scherenschnitte. Many of this folk art's traditions—passed from generation to generation by word of mouth—were never recorded. Thousands of actual cuttings have been lost to time: early inks ate away at the paper they embellished, and the pioneers of papercutting frequently discarded their work. Even treasured cuttings, stored in family Bibles or in albums, were misplaced. Nevertheless, bits and pieces of tantalizing historical information emerge—from surviving cut work (much of it now in private collections and museums), from research, and from the papercutting stories that are told and retold through time.

Paper was invented in China around A.D. 200. At some time during the fourth or fifth century, the Chinese started to cut paper embroidery patterns. Though these first artists were probably members of the royal entourage, papercutting quickly became a folk art, one practiced not by royalty but by commoners. Their cut work served both decorative and utilitarian purposes.

Cut paper patterns were used to place patterns on textiles and porcelains and to dye materials. Similar cut-outs played a part in funeral rites; paper replicas of the deceased's belongings were burned so that they would follow their owner into the afterlife. Paper was cut for purely decorative purposes as well. Homes were (and still are) hung with paper cut-outs, especially during festivals. Today, cut paper designs are exchanged as gifts or greetings. Shantung province, famous for its silks, is particularly well-known for this custom.

Contemporary Chinese cuttings are often based on patterns centuries old and are usually cut on flat rather than folded paper. While some artists create their own designs, many pride themselves on being able to copy traditional patterns exactly. The familiar symbols and figures that appear in their cut work are as old as papercutting itself: fish, flowers, lanterns, dragons, birds, and images drawn from familiar folk tales.

Chinese papercutters use different sets of tools and distinct techniques to create their intricate cut work. Some use large, oval-handled scissors with short, sharp blades. The artist incises and cuts interior lines first and then cuts the exterior borders by making one long, continuous sweep with the scissors.

The second Chinese method of cutting, an ancient one that is still practiced, allows a single cutter to make many cuttings simultaneously. First, the bottom of an open wooden box is covered with a mixture of fat and charcoal. This hardened cutting surface lasts for years and serves to prevent knife blades from being dulled. Each time cutting is about to commence, the artist scrapes this surface clean and coats it with a light dusting of flour. A stack of tissue-thin papers—sometimes as many as 50 or 60—is then placed flat within the frame; the flour prevents the bottom sheet from sticking to the cutting surface. Usually, a pattern is placed on top of the stack, but some professional cutters work without one. All the sheets are held in place with nails or large stitches. Knives, chisels, stamps, and punches—often handmade—are then used to cut through the top pattern lines and down through all the layers underneath. Great skill is required to do this accurately.

Yet another technique, used by women in Shantung, begins with a professionally cut stencil pattern. The pattern is cut out and placed on a sheet of paper. Both are dampened with water, pressed together, and held over a smoking lamp. When the papers have thoroughly dried, the pattern is pulled off. The remaining piece of paper—with its white and black areas clearly defined—is sewn to a stack of colored papers. By cutting along the visible pattern lines with scissors and knives, the artist is able to cut through all the sheets simultaneously.

There are also artists who cut single sheets, one at a time, with a knife blade only. This blade resembles the craft knives used by contemporary European cutters but is traditionally made by hand. Today, unfortunately, commercial Chinese cut work is sometimes made by machines which stamp out thousands of identical cut pieces. Hand-cut paper is still widely available, however.

Separated from their Chinese counterparts by thousands of miles, the Maya of Central America developed a paper-like substance during the sixth century. Made from the inner bark of the wild fig tree, this *amate*, as it is known, was widely used in ancient Mexico. It is still used—and probably has been for centuries—by the Otomi Indians, who cut symmetrical paper votive figures from it. Though Otomi cuttings are far less sophisticated in design than the cuttings of Asia and Europe and are now made largely for the tourist trade, they still play an integral role in religious rituals and magic rites.

When villagers visit a *brujo* or *bruja* (male or female witch), they bring a packet of amate paper, which the brujo cuts into figures called *munecos*. When these figures are cut from light-colored paper, they represent the forces of good; when they're cut from dark-colored paper, they represent the forces of evil. White paper cut-outs are buried along with the dead, figure prominently

OPPOSITE PAGE *Chinese cut work*

ABOVE *Traditional papercut amate figures play an important role in Otomi religious rituals and magic rites.*

9 ◆

Birds are a popular motif in cuttings from many countries. These colorful examples were cut in China.

in planting and harvest rites, and are used in healing rituals as well. Dark figures are equally powerful. When a village woman gossips too much, chewing gum is pressed over the mouth of a dark figure cut to resemble her!

By the seventh century, papercutting had spread from China to Japan. Samurai warriors—proud members of the Japanese military caste—embellished their armor with many different designs. *Mon-kiri*, the Japanese art of papercutting, was used to cut these same emblems and crests from paper. Cut work also served to identify family belongings and to transfer patterns to textiles.

Mon-kiri was gradually abandoned as the art of folding paper (origami) became more widespread, but the Japanese are still famous for their papercut stencils. These are used in *katazome*—the ancient Japanese art of stencil dyeing.

The concept of creating symmetrically cut designs, by folding paper before cutting it, may have originated in Japan. Certainly, Japanese art reflects an interest in the symmetry of nature. The chrysanthemum, which is the flower of Japan's imperial crest and which frequently appears as a motif in painting and in mon-kiri, is portrayed with sixteen geometrical petals.

From Asia, the knowledge of paper and cut work spread gradually along trade routes until it reached the Middle East, probably during the eighth century. By the 1500s, Turkey could boast of a guild devoted exclusively to the task of papercutting. When this guild's members filed past the Sultan during a ceremony in 1582, one observer noted that they displayed a portable garden made entirely of cut paper flowers.

Paper making—and cutting—eventually filtered into Europe, and by the seventeenth century, papercutters in Italy, Holland, Germany, and Switzerland were developing distinct regional cutting styles. Much of the early cut work from all of these countries was religious in nature. Because paper was still made by hand and was therefore costly, most of it was reserved for use in monasteries. Cloistered monks and nuns painstakingly created hand-lettered and painted religious texts, some of which boasted papercut designs as well. Both lettering and painted figures and scenes were enhanced with elaborate cut work. The magnificent *Book of Passion*, which was made around 1500 for King Henry VII of England, incorporated cut designs on every vellum page.

In addition to these stunning texts, smaller religious cuttings were created and exchanged in northern Germany on Holy Days. These were also presented as gifts at confirmations. The folded and cut sheets were so common that they came to be known as *prayer papers*. Religious themes continued to play a major role in papercutting, even after cut work was no longer practiced exclusively in monasteries.

Not all European cut work was religious in nature. Early European papercuttings were used in a number of ways. Paper stencils were used in medieval churches to create decorative painted borders on walls. These papercut designs were first lacquered or oiled to prevent them from absorbing paint and then held directly against the surfaces to be painted. The designs with which they were cut were often based on traditional patterns from Asia and North Africa.

Once the printing press was invented, pattern books full of stencil designs were circulated throughout Europe. Wood craftsmen found that these stencil patterns could be used to create veneers. In fact, until the late seventeenth century, many patterns—in furniture, embroidery, and stencilled art—could be traced back to their papercutting origins.

Untitled

Jan de Bleijker

Cut in 1762, this astounding piece portrays specific Biblical verses, one in each circle. Clockwise from top left: Ruth 2:10; Acts 11:10; Gen. 24:19; Luke 15:21; Acts 27:43; John 5.4, Jonah 1.17, Luke 25.13.

By the seventeenth century, German and Swiss scherenschnitte had become a folk art form. Cutting techniques varied. Many cut-outs were created from single-folded paper; others were cut from flat sheets. The Swiss also developed a method of layering cut paper, though collage was not their predominant technique. Most scherenschnitte was cut from black or white paper and depended on contour rather than color for its effect.

During the seventeenth century, the Swiss—and other Europeans— cut impressively elaborate designs on many of their legal documents. Professional scriveners (or writers) embellished these documents with cut work, glued them to fabric or expensive paper, and then rolled or folded them for safe-keeping. The packages were sometimes sealed with paper shapes remaining from the original cutting. Cut work not only made documents attractive but was very difficult to falsify or replicate illegally; each scrivener's cutting style was so distinct that the designs served as a kind of personal signature. The Swiss also cut greeting cards on folded and on flat paper and were famed for their papercut bookmarks. *Marques* is still the Swiss word for paper cut-outs.

One Germanic form of cut work, which was later brought to the United States by emigrating members of religious sects, was the hand-cut valentine. Some were amazingly elaborate; cut-out doors revealed flowers, hearts, and cupids as well as hand-lettered words of love. Not until the invention of the paper-embossing machine did the practice of making these paper messages begin to fade away.

Papercutting arrived in Holland during the early 1600s and may have been brought by Portuguese Jewish immigrants to that country. It was quickly and enthusiastically adopted as a folk art. Much early Dutch cut work, like cut art in other European countries, served to embellish religious, legal, and commemorative documents. Interestingly, the cut embellishments on these papers often occupied three or four times as much space as the written or cut text on them.

By the late seventeenth and early eighteenth centuries, some cut pieces were so finely detailed that

Frederick (II) the Great of Prussia

Jhr. van Suchtelen (1722-1788)

During the eighteenth century, some cuttings were so intricate that they looked more like paintings or drawings.

they looked almost like paintings. Early attempts by papercutters to imitate more graphic art forms gave way, however, to imaginative cutting styles, in which the cutter focused more intently on contour than on artificially created effects of light and shading.

Contemporary Dutch papercutters are among the finest in the world. Their work is characterized by its spontaneity and variety, rather than by any single regional style. Although many Dutch artists use scissors and cut on flat or folded paper, there are as many different forms, subjects, and techniques in Dutch cut work as there are cutters. Since the 1600s, Dutch artists have used knives as well as scissors; paper carving is known as *schneiden.*

Jews throughout Europe and the Middle East were also dedicated papercutters. With the near total destruction of Jewish life in Europe, their folk art almost disappeared, but a few surviving pieces illustrate the rich history of Jewish cut work. Traditionally (but not always) cut by men and boys, elegant Jewish cut-outs—often cut on single-folded paper—bore pictorial symbols directly related to the Old Testament and to the Torah. Menorahs (the seven-armed candelabra), the Tablets of the Law, the Torah crown (representing God), and Stars of David were common in many cuttings.

Cut paper mizrahs were hung on the east walls in homes and synagogues. (East is the direction faced during evening prayers.) Marriage contracts (or Ketuboh) were carved with ornate designs, and the religious festival of Shavuot inspired cut-outs known as *shevuoslech* and *raizelech.* Hebrew text was also painstakingly incorporated in many of these cuttings. One astounding Italian piece of the early seventeenth century takes the form of a lengthy scroll upon which is cut the Old Testament story of Esther.

Handmade Jewish cut work is less common now than it once was, though contemporary papercutters in Europe, North Africa, Turkey, and the United States do continue with the magnificent traditions of their ancestors. In Israel, at recent exhibitions, cut pieces created by immigrants from several different countries displayed a surprising similarity in subjects and styles.

Untitled

I.G. Kerp-Schlesinger

The first of these two humorous cuttings is a family portrait. The artist's husband directs. Under his baton stands the cutter, looking— she claims—not quite as beautiful as she did when she was twenty-five. Each of her children "plays a different instrument." The second cutting resulted from a stay in the hospital. Included are a violinist (to drown out the artist's screams), a physician holding a hypodermic syringe, a pharmacist with his mortar and pestle, and a devilish nurse taking blood samples.

Tzion Halo Tishali

Tamar Fishman

This contemporary cutting includes Hebrew text: "O Zion, wilt thou not ask if peace be with thy captives, that seek thy peace, that are the remnants of thy flocks?" (Judah Halevi, 1086-1141).

Only the ornamentation on these traditionally cut pieces demonstrated significant differences.

By the eighteenth and nineteenth centuries, papercutting was fairly common throughout Europe, and while religious themes were still prevalent, cut work included heraldic designs, birds, flowers, and figures from mythology. German fairy tales were also illustrated with cut-out pictures. Even Hans Christian Andersen, the famous Danish fairy tale writer, tried his hand at cutting.

An especially widespread form of cut work was the art of *silhouette* cutting. These paper profiles were an inexpensive alternative to expensive painted portraits, which few people could afford. Cut from black or white paper, they were named for a much disliked French Minister of Finance, Etienne de Silhouette, who held office during the reign of Louis XV. His miserly attempts to keep government spending under control gave birth to the word silhouette, which quickly come to mean anything done inexpensively.

Silhouettes were made by casting a shadow of the subject's profile against a wall, tracing the shadow, and then cutting out the traced outline. The completed cutting was filled in with black paint or ink. With the invention of the pantograph, silhouette artists were able to reduce the shadow's size mechanically, but before that time, some skilled artists didn't even use a traced shadow image; they simply studied their subjects and then cut. Itinerant papercutters travelled from village to village, cutting likenesses of entire families. When business was slow, they turned to papercuttings of trees, flowers, birds, and human figures instead.

Once photography was invented, silhouette cutting faded in popularity, but before the camera existed, thousands of people delighted in this popular hobby. From locket-sized, miniature profiles of loved ones to life-sized framed pieces, silhouettes were made in almost every European papercutting country.

In England, as elsewhere in Europe, papercutting during the eighteenth and nineteenth centuries was extremely popular. Making silhouettes and "paper mosaicks" were favorite pastimes, and cut-outs were carefully saved in family albums. Two famous papercutters of this period, Mary Delaney and Amelia Blackburn, did much to legitimize papercutting as an art form.

Mrs. Mary Delaney (1700-1788) made astoundingly beautiful paper mosaics. From small, cut pieces of colored paper, this talented artist created two-dimensional flowers so

ABOVE The Amish of Dresdan, New York, *22" (55.9 cm) x 28" (71.1 cm), © 1983, Marie-Helene Grabman*

Traditional subject matter in a fine contemporary cutting

LEFT Purim Story, *16" (40.6 cm) x 16" (40.6 cm), © 1990, Dan Howarth*

Pisces, the fish, is a symbol for the Hebrew month during which Purim takes place. Like Jewish history, the fish swims in circles. Within the circle are the words, "For the Jews there was light and happiness and joy and honor; in every nation…there was rejoicing and gladness, a day of feasting and goodness."

ABOVE Untitled

Hans Christian Andersen

RIGHT *Silhouettes of Schiller, Goethe, E. Haines, and Rothschild cut by I.G. Kerp-Schlesinger*

lifelike that they stand among the finest botanical representations—as well as cuttings—ever made. More remarkable yet is the fact that Mrs. Delaney didn't start to cut paper until she was in her seventies; she stopped only when she lost her sight at age eighty-two. One of her most avid fans was Princess Elizabeth—the third daughter of King George III—who was an enthusiastic papercutter herself.

Amelia Blackburn was a renowned Victorian papercutter who worked during the 1830s. An invalid, Mrs. Blackburn combined a number of papercutting techniques: symmetrical cutting, collage, painting, and pin pricking. Her work was so greatly admired that cut pieces during the Victorian era were often called "Amelias."

In Poland, paper cut-outs (or *wycinanki*) were probably in existence long before the nineteenth century, but the earliest known Polish cut work dates from the mid 1800s. Though it's assumed that the first Polish papercutters inherited their art form from neighboring European countries, there is some evidence to suggest that Polish peasants were simply continuing a long-lived tradition—that of cutting designs in the sheepskin coverings of their cottage windows.

In any event, papercutters in Poland not only continued the tradition of symmetrical cutting, but added another as well—the layering of colorful, cut

Schiller Goethe E. Haines Rothschild

paper pieces to form pictorial collages. And unlike their counterparts in western Europe, Polish cutters rarely cut for any reason other than pleasure; wycinanki are purely decorative.

During the early 1900s, when the use of paper spread to Poland's rural areas, a true folk art was born. Ebullient, colorful, and cheerful, Polish paper cut-outs were fashioned from any paper available to the farmers and peasants who cut them: scraps of writing paper, colored papers, tissue, and thin cardboard. These were hung from the rafters of cottages, pasted on newly white-washed walls, and used as decorations at Christmas and Easter. Designs were cut without preliminary sketching.

Two distinct, regional cutting styles developed in and around Warsaw. One style was born in Kurpie (north of Warsaw) and the other in Lowicz (south-west of Warsaw). Kurpie work is often cut from a single, dark-colored piece of paper (either circular or rectangular), folded lengthwise. The single-folded types, called *leluje*, usually include a symmetrical and central tree form—probably based on the pagan symbol for the tree of life—and one or more pairs of birds. The circular types are called *gwiazda* (stars) and are folded and cut so that their patterns are repeated eight, sixteen, or thirty-two times.

Lowicz papercuttings, on the other hand, are most often comprised of a basic black cutting with cut, colored pieces layered on it. Among the designs found on Lowicz gwiazda, floral arrangements with roosters are quite com-

CLOCKWISE FROM UPPER LEFT: *Luise Duttenhofer, Moritz von Schwindt, Dr. Georg Plischke, Hans Seidel* (Fleeing from the Damaged Environment).

Cuttings are effective as protests.

The hunting scene decries wealthy landlords who trampled through poor peasants' leased land.

Wagner's music is belittled in the contemporary Dutch cutting filled with cats.

A German artist, who despised the National Socialist Party's emphasis on "manly virtue," cut a scathing commentary over an upturned sword in 1932: "Wretched are the people who forget that peace is manly virtue."

The title of the cut animals piece speaks for itself.

Cutwork Valentine, *13" (33 cm) diameter, unidentified artist (possibly W. Chand...), circa 1753. Watercolor and ink on laid paper. 57.306.1; T90-327. Courtesy of the Abby Aldrich Rockefeller Folk Art Center, Williamsburg, Virginia.*

This papercut valentine is one of the earliest surviving American scherenschnitte of its type. The following verses are inscribed on its arcs:

*This morning as I lay in bed'
Engaged in thoughtfull muse,
It gently came into my head
A Valentine to choose.*

*Swift as the fleeting thts (thoughts) of man
My roving fancy flew,
And of bright nymphs a numero (= us clan)
Presented to my view.
Long time in deep suspence I stood
Before I gave my voice,
At length resolv('')d this fair one should
Determine my choice,
One quite averse to envious hate,
Hypocrisy and pride,
In all the methods of deceit
And calumny untry'd,
But all my searches were in vain,
Without the least exception,
For none among the blooming train*

*Wou'd answer the description (.)
Despairing of success I cry'd
Not one this title bless-
There is my friendly muse reply'd
Her name it is: E. S.*

Oral tradition has it that E. S. was Elizabeth Sandwith, who in 1761 married a fellow Philadelphia Quaker, Henry Drinker. Mr. Drinker did not cut this Valentine, however. The signature of the original artist (and rejected suitor) was deliberately obliterated. All that remains of the inscription is (illeg.) Chand. (illeg.) to E:S: February 14, 1753."

mon. *Kodry* designs, on a long horizontal axis, feature fantastic, decorative flowers and birds or portray everyday scenes from village life. Because they require so much time to make, kodry are quite difficult to find today. Another popular motif of the Lowicz region is a layered rosette and streamer shape. Ribbons much like these paper versions were worn from men's belts. Their designs were specific to their owners' homes—so specific that anyone familiar with the design could quickly tell where the owner lived.

Polish cut work is usually made with scissors, but a few papercutters actually carve their paper designs with sheep shears! This practice originated during a time when Russian invaders confiscated all small knives and scissors. Intrepid Polish villagers simply trained themselves to cut paper with unwieldy shears instead and became so adept that the tradition was continued. Wycinanki cut with shears are simply amazing in their intricacy.

Scherenschnitte was carried to America by immigrants who came from southern Germany and Switzerland during the late seventeenth century. Many of these settlers in America were fleeing from religious persecution in their homelands. The Mennonites, Seventh Day Baptists of Ephrata, Moravians of Bethlehem, Schwenkfelders, and members of the Lutheran and Reformed faiths brought with them not only papercutting skills and tools but a wealth of religious imagery and a love of color and design as well. The areas in which these people settled—Lancaster County, Pennsylvania, is probably the best known—are still centers of papercutting artistry today.

ABOVE The Ribbons, *18" (45.7 cm) x 30" (76.2 cm), © 1991, Elżbieta Kaleta. These paper ribbons were cut and layered in the Lowicz regional style and are very similar to the painted or embroidered ribbons attached to Polish folk costumes.*

LEFT Adam and Eve, *10" (25.4 cm) x 11-3/8 (28.8 cm), © 1983, Sandra Gilpin. Some of today's finest papercutters have adopted and revitalized the traditions of long ago. This charming cut-out makes wonderful use of the religious imagery, painting, and fraktur so popular in Pennsylvania scherenschnitte two centuries ago.*

Because paper was costly and in short supply in America, just as it was in Europe, its use was initially limited to significant papers: illuminated religious texts, legal documents, birth certificates (*geburtschein*), baptismal certificates (*taufschein*), and confirmation and marriage certificates (*trauschein*). These documents were often additionally embellished with painting and *fraktur*, a type of German hand-lettering named for its broken or fractured appearance. Accomplished fraktur artists in the United States continued the traditional work of their forefathers for some time. But once in awhile, possibly because no fraktur artist was available, documents were embellished with cut work instead.

Some of the earliest known papercuttings in North America were created by members of the Seventh Day Baptist Society at the Ephrata Cloister in Ephrata, Pennsylvania. During the eighteenth century, this community operated its own paper mill, and some of its members were gifted fraktur artists. One sister of that society, who was asked to submit an illuminated page for a hymnal, but who didn't share the painting and lettering talents of her peers, designed a cut paper pattern instead.

The skill and vision of Pennsylvania German and Dutch papercutting was most apparent, however, in early American *liebesbriefe* (love letters). Some of the few that survive are so extraordinary that it's difficult to imagine how any woman could have rejected the papercutting suitors who made them. Symmetrically cut, then painted, inked, and sometimes pin-pricked as well, the exquisitely designed and lettered pieces inspired a vogue for valentine making during Victorian times. Later valentines, however, rarely approached the complexity of these earlier versions, some of which constituted complete marriage proposals.

Pictorial symbols were common in these and other Pennsylvania German scherenschnitte pieces. The heart shape that appeared in so many papercuttings represented both the heart of God and God as a source of love and hope. On marriage certificates, the lettered names of the happy couple were inked within a heart shape to suggest that the couple would be surrounded by God's love. The tulip was a symbol of man's search for God, and flowers with three petals stood for the Holy Trinity. Birds of all sorts were thought to have spiritual significance. The distelfink represented the Holy Spirit and was also a symbol of good luck. The turtle dove symbolized the soul's yearning for Christ, and peacocks represented eternity.

As paper became less difficult to obtain, and as scissors started to be imported from Europe, papercutting extended into daily life as well. Frugal housewives lined their shelves with *faltschnittbander*, long sheets of paper with decorative cut designs on their overhanging borders. During the late nineteenth century, *orange papers*, the tissues in which fruit was wrapped, were used to make doilies. These were placed under oil lamps, dishes, and baked goods. Circles of clean, cut paper were placed on top of butter in dishes and crocks. Children cut paper Christmas decorations, and silhouettes became just as popular as they were in Europe. Paper stencils were used to paint patterns on walls, bedspreads, tablecloths, and floor coverings. Papercut designs, too, began to reflect the designs of everyday life: quilt and embroidery patterns, the carvings on blanket chests, needlework patterns, and the elaborate metalwork on grills and gates.

Fishing in the Rio Grande

23" (58.4 cm) x 31" (78.7 cm)

© 1989, Elżbieta Kaleta

This amazingly intricate piece was cut with scissors. The cutter has blended her traditional, Polish papercutting skills with motifs from her present home in the southwestern United States.

Unfortunately, few early American cut pieces are still in existence. They were often stored within the pages of the family Bible—the only book a household was likely to own. As family members separated, and as time passed, the Bibles—and their precious contents—were lost. Most of the cut pieces that survive are now in private collections and museums. Their makers, who rarely signed their work, are often unknown.

As machine-cut and stamped paper began to take the place of hand-cut art, papercutting waned. During the early part of this century, its popularity was at an ebb. Nevertheless, dedicated cutting artists all over the world nurtured their craft; they maintained its traditions and continued to add new perspectives and styles of their own. Within the past few decades, a new generation of papercutters has combined the best aspects of traditional papercutting with amazing new content and materials, and papercutting has been reborn as an international art form. Guilds are once again active, collectors now seek excellent cut work, and thousands of novice papercutters are joining the ranks of enthusiastic converts to the long-lived world of cut paper art.

PAPERCUTTING:

BASIC TECHNIQUES

As our papercutting ancestors discovered, you don't need years of formal training or a huge bank balance to cut paper successfully. You do need time to practice, but by the time you've finished reading this section, you'll be well on your way to making papercuttings of which you can be proud. Many of today's renowned cutting artists started just as you are starting, with nothing more than curiosity, enthusiasm, and patience. As their cutting hands became more nimble, and as they mastered basic techniques, their imaginations began to give shape to unique visions and new styles. The same capabilities and the same discoveries await you.

Papercutting techniques differ, but the basic steps to creating cut work—all cut work—are exactly the same. Whether you plan to cut a simple, no-fold bookmark design, create an intricate, multi-folded doily, or layer cut paper in a colorful collage, you'll need to select paper, transfer a pattern to it, and cut along the pattern lines. Once you understand these essential steps, mastering the variations that make papercutting such a fascinating art form will be easy. You'll soon be designing, folding, cutting, painting, staining, and embellishing cuttings of your own.

In the meantime, let the learning process be a playful one. Don't let your imagination be squelched by "rules." Some are important, of course; this section will introduce you to most of them. Others exist only to be broken. As you read, stop to experiment. Try new folds, new cuts, and new embellishments. Then sweep your mistakes into the trash and enjoy your successes.

SETTING UP SHOP

Papercutting lacks only one thing: snob appeal. In fact, if you're expecting your friends to exclaim in surprise over your fabulously equipped studio, you might want to consider a future in antique restoration instead. Your papercutting workshop is likely to be invisible when you aren't actually "in" it; most of your materials will fit into a couple of kitchen drawers. You won't be showing off elaborate

equipment either. There isn't much of it, and what you will need is inexpensive. Never mind. The admiration that your cut work demands will more than compensate!

Skim the list of tools and equipment. Check around the house before you run out to buy anything. Many of the required items are likely to be ones you already own. If you're a beginner, don't worry about buying fancy paper yet either; just grab yesterday's newspaper or a few sheets of typing paper. Clear off the kitchen table, pour yourself a cup of tea or coffee, and settle in to read the rest of this section. As you learn more about how each item is used, you'll have a much better sense of when and where to buy it.

Almost any paper is suitable for cut work.

What you won't need

A closet full of expensive equipment and supplies
A large, well-furnished work space
Years of intensive training

What you can't do without

Choose one:

Surgical scissors

Embroidery scissors

Manicure scissors

Craft knife and #11 blades with mat board, linoleum,
or an empty, flattened, cereal box

Pencil
Paper
Masking tape, "invisible" tape, or a stapler
Two hours to read this section
Patience and a sense of humor

What you'll need for a truly sophisticated workshop

Starting equipment and personal qualities already listed
More paper
Glue
Needle and thread
Compass
Tea bags or instant coffee
Cosmetic sponge
Watercolors and brushes
Pen and ink
Small cup or bowl
Spoon
Waxed paper
Heavy book or iron
Blank stationery and envelopes
Tracing paper
Graphite paper or transfer paper
Metal ruler
Push pins
Hole punch

SELECTING PAPER

Paper is a renewable resource, but it won't be renewable in the future unless we all protect its sources—Mother Nature and her trees. As you choose paper and as you cut it, gently remind yourself that your caring stewardship will make our world a healthier, more productive, and longer-lived environment for future generations. Purchase recycled paper when you can and practice with newspapers or scraps. Sweep up any bits that are too small to use and deliver them to your local recycling center.

You'll be in good company if you choose only one or two types of paper for all of your cuttings. Some of today's best papercutters do just that. Parchment paper is a popular choice because it folds and irons well, accepts paints and stains, can be easily cut even when it's folded, and is durable. Bond and calligraphy paper have similar qualities. If experimentation and decision-making fill you with dread, choose a single paper and master it, but if you yearn to explore the wonderful world of paper, here are some guidelines to help you along the way.

Choosing an appropriate paper is as simple as understanding your project itself. Its design, its intended use, and its appearance will quickly guide you toward some paper possibilities and just as quickly away from others.

Study your pattern's folding requirements first. Will you be cutting from a single, flat sheet, or will the paper be folded? It's fairly easy to cut through a single layer of thick, heavy paper, but if the same paper is folded several times, attempts to cut through all the layers may cause your cutting hand to go on strike.

Busy Day in the Mimbres Valley
29" (73.7 cm) x 29" (73.7 cm)
© 1991, Elżbieta Kaleta
Cut with scissors on a single sheet of flat paper

If your pattern requires folding, be sure to choose a paper that will retain a crisp fold while you work. Folds that slip while you cut cause the finished piece to be asymmetrical. If you're planning to frame and display a folded design, check to see that your paper doesn't hold a fold even better than you'd like. The slick surfaces on some papers crack when they're folded; no amount of ironing will erase the evidence. Of course, these marks won't show—or matter—on standing, three-dimensional pieces, but they might look unsightly on others.

Then look at the pattern lines. Are they delicate and ornate or simple and robust? A traditional, layered, Polish rooster design might call for a paper as colorful and solid as the bird itself. A delicate, multi-folded doily in the same paper—assuming you could even cut it—would probably look silly.

How do you plan to use your cut work? Delicate tissue papers—protected by frames—will last at least as long as you do. The life-span of a tissue bookmark, however, wouldn't be worth measuring. At times, durability won't be of any concern at all. German immigrants in America used papercut newspapers to line shelves. As soon as these short-lived strips were torn or soiled, they were replaced. Select colored papers carefully; some varieties fade with exposure to sunlight.

Will you be applying paint, ink, or stain to your project? Water colors and inks may bleed on very porous paper. Stains won't be absorbed very well by

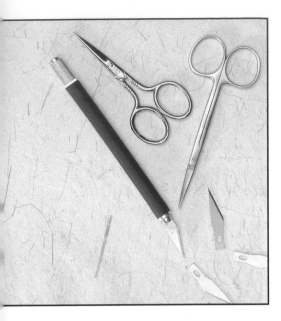

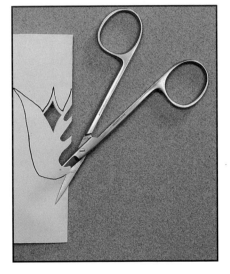

TOP *Surgical scissors, manicure scissors, and craft knives are all suitable cutting implements.*

BOTTOM *Starting a cut at the apex of the blades*

OPPOSITE PAGE, TOP *Cut interior portions first.*

OPPOSITE PAGE, BOTTOM *Protect thin paper by stapling it between two sheets of heavier paper. Transfer the pattern to the top sheet and cut through all layers simultaneously.*

papers with slick surfaces and will cause some colored papers to run. Save paper (and time) by experimenting before you begin the actual project.

What kinds of paper are available in your area? Take a trip through your local paper or arts supply store. Don't be afraid to ask questions of the salespeople there or to ask for free samples. Choose a few different papers that appeal to you, take them home, and—after you've finished this section—play with them. Fold and iron, paint and stain, cut and cut and cut. The more experience you gain with each type of paper, the more quickly you'll master the art of paper selection.

TIPS:

■ Antique-colored parchment paper is available at some crafts stores and printing shops.

■ If paper suppliers are sparse in your area, try your local printing or copy shops.

■ Beautiful handmade papers may be available through individual paper makers in your area.

■ When you first start papercutting, it's a good idea to practice with dark, non-glossy papers. Glossy papers distract your attention from the contours of your cut edges. Dark papers emphasize them, so you'll be able to see your cut edges clearly. If you can't find dark paper, go ahead and use white paper but cut against a dark background so that your cut lines will be visible.

Listed below are some of the papers most commonly used by papercutting artists. Parchment and calligraphy paper are good choices for the beginner.

Parchment paper
Calligraphy paper
Bond
Tissue paper
Rice Paper
Flint-coated paper
Foil

CUTTING TOOLS AND TECHNIQUES

Most of us would probably nip off a precious finger or two if we tried to imitate Polish papercutters, who sometimes cut paper with sheep shears! Surgical scissors and craft knives are safe alternatives.

As your read the sections that follow, keep in mind that there are two sides to a cut sheet of paper. The side that will be displayed will be the side that is unmarked by any remaining pattern lines.

Scissors

When you set out to buy scissors, look for a pair that have small blades and sharp points. They should be small enough to make delicate twists and turns in the paper, pointed enough to start tiny cuts in the center of intricate patterns, and strong enough to cut through multiple layers. Surgical scissors are the best choice for the serious papercutter; the blades are remarkably sharp and perfectly aligned. Inexpensive alternatives include embroidery, manicure, and small sewing scissors.

Scissoring techniques vary. Most papercutters move the paper—not their scissors—as they cut. This is an especially effective method when working with sharp angles and tight curves. A few papercutters prefer to move their scissors but not the paper. Try this when you're cutting sweeping curves and straight lines. (Obviously, you'll have to adjust the paper at some point.)

Notice which part of the scissors you use. Usually, you should start cuts with the portion of the blades closest to their apex and finish the cut without closing the blades completely. Closing the blades to their pointed ends is likely to leave ragged edges along cut lines. Remember, though, that you're the only person who can decide which method of cutting is best for you. By all means choose a method that's comfortable and alter it to suit the pattern that you're cutting.

Begin by making the smallest, inside cuts first. Cutting out interior sections is difficult if you've already cut away so much paper around them that you have nothing left to grasp with your non-cutting hand. Start these interior cuts by puncturing the paper with the points of your scissors—near to, but not on, the cutting line. Cut from the puncture point out toward the line and then follow the line. Outside edges should be cut last.

TIPS:

- Always keep the blades sharp. The tiniest of nicks on a blade will force your hand to exert extra pressure when the nicked part touches the paper. Then, once the damaged section of the blade has passed through the paper, you won't be able to stop the rest of the blade from moving through too quickly. That unexpected rush of cutting as your scissors close may cause you to overshoot your pattern lines!

- Open the blades before you pull your scissors away from a completed cut. If the blades are closed, they may pull paper along with them.

- If you find that your scissors start to bend the paper, especially when you're cutting sharp curves, try cutting from below the paper instead of from above.

- When cutting very delicate lines, support flimsy paper sections by placing a thicker sheet of paper below the thin one you are cutting. Cut through both sheets simultaneously.

Craft knives

Craft knives are particularly effective on thick, multi-folded papers, but some artists use them for all cutting. They're relatively easy to manipulate, and their razor-sharp blades are inexpensive to replace.

Always protect your craft knife blade, your cutting paper, and your work surface by placing a protective piece of mat board, non-corrugated card-board, linoleum, or similar, semi-rigid material underneath your paper. An unfolded, empty cereal box will work well too. Trying to cut without this added protection will leave you with a lot of dull blades and a permanently scarred work surface. Blades tend to drag on rigid surfaces; when they do, they're likely to snag.

As you cut shapes with a craft knife, remind yourself to stop the blade just as it meets its finishing point. If you stop the blade too soon and try to lift the cut section away, the paper may tear as you pull on it. If you cut too far, the cut marks may show on your finished design.

One popular technique is to feed the paper into the knife blade, moving the paper rather than the blade. Press the point of the blade into the pattern line, with the cutting edge of the blade facing you, and then carefully guide the paper into the blade with your free hand. Hold the forefinger of your non-cutting hand over delicate areas to keep the paper from tearing as you cut.

In order to minimize paper motion, cut all vertical lines at the same time and then shift the paper so that you can cut all the horizontal lines. Use a metal ruler when cutting straight lines.

Plenty of practice (see patterns on opposite page) will help you to master your craft knife blade.

Whether you use a knife or scissors, practice, practice, and practice some more! Cutting without pattern lines to guide you is an excellent way to learn to manipulate your scissors or craft knife. Choose a pattern that you like and try to replicate it without transferring the pattern—just let your eyes guide your cutting hand. Cutting repetitive shapes also increases dexterity and speed. Cut several rows of triangles on the folded edges of scrap paper. See how quickly and how accurately you can cut each triangle to match the next.

When you're new to cutting and design, it's sometimes wise to start by cutting just the basic outlines of the pattern you have in mind. Once you've learned to see and cut those, you can elaborate on your first, simple version by adding details. The butterfly below has been cut three separate times, and each time, the artist has added more elaborate designs.

TIPS:

- Use the pointed edge of the blade to cut curves and the straight edge to cut straight lines.

- Once you've completed a cut, you can use the tip of your blade to stab and lift away the scrap.

- Don't try to turn the paper or the blade around a sharp angle. When you reach an angled point on the cutting line, lift your blade, move the paper, and begin cutting again

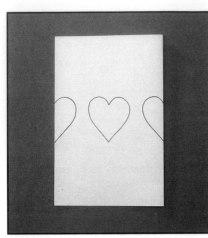

Photo 1

Photo 2

Pins and hole punches

Amelia Blackburn, a nineteenth-century English papercutter, was famous for her pin-pricked cut work. The technique she made so popular is really quite simple. After you've ironed and embellished your papercutting, turn it upside-down and place it on a firm but porous surface; foam or felt will do. Make holes by inserting an ordinary push pin through the back of the cutting. Hole sizes can be varied by inserting different kinds (and sizes) of pins or by inserting one pin to different depths.

The slightly raised surfaces around these holes add texture to the finished cutting. If you'd rather not raise the front of the paper's surface, just insert the pin from the front of the paper instead. No matter how you create these holes, when you hold a pin-pricked design up to light, the effect will be quite dramatic.

Standard, one-hole punches will generate perfectly matched, larger holes and will save your wrist from unnecessary gymnastics!

TIPS:

■ Chinese papercutters used pins to "draw" pattern lines on multiple layers of paper. They first arranged several layers of paper in a box, the edges of which kept the sheets aligned. A pattern was placed on top of this stack of paper, and a pin was inserted at regular intervals along the pattern lines. The hundreds of resulting pinholes, which pierced every sheet, were clearly visible when the sheets were removed and served as pattern lines.

FOLDING

Folding paper before cutting it serves two purposes: it allows the papercutter to save time (cuts are repeated on other portions of the folded paper), and it creates symmetry (a single pattern is repeated in predictable and balanced ways). Paper can be folded once (a single fold), twice (a double fold), three times (a triple fold), or more times (multiple folds). Folds can be made on rectangular, square, circular, or irregularly shaped papers. Each of these folding patterns results in a different design layout.

It's entirely possible to create stunning cut work without understanding one bit of folding theory; simple instructions are almost always provided with commercial patterns. You'll also find that many cuttings are made without any folds at all. Some understanding of when and why paper is folded, however, will allow you to adapt designs and to create one-of-a-kind patterns of your own.

The step-by-step folding lessons provided here include a series of practice sessions.

Note that cutting lines should be drawn with a sharp, soft pencil. Solid black cutting lines are used in illustrations only to show the cutting lines clearly.

What you'll need

Scrap paper—plenty of it!
Scissors or craft knife and mat board
Compass
Pencil
Ruler
Masking tape, invisible tape, or a stapler

Single Folds

By cutting along the pattern lines on one half of a folded piece of paper, you can create a mirror image of that pattern on the paper's opposite half. Circular and irregularly shaped papers are just as easily folded as square or rectangular ones.

Fold a single sheet of paper in half. Be sure that the fold is crisp and that the top and bottom edges line up evenly. With a pencil, draw one half of a heart along the folded edge. Now draw another half of a heart along any unfolded edge. Next draw a complete heart in the center of the paper; its starting and finishing points should meet without touching any of the paper's edges. See Photo 1.

Then hold or tape the folded halves firmly together. Using either scissors or a craft knife, cut out all three patterns. Unfold to see the completed pattern, as shown in Photo 2.

The half heart which was drawn along the folded edge is now joined to its mirror image. The half heart drawn at an uncut edge, however, repeats itself on an opposite or adjacent edge of the paper. The third heart, cut in the paper's center, has produced two discrete designs, each ringed by paper.

Fold another sheet of paper in half. Then draw a whole heart along the folded edge. (Be sure to draw this heart so that a small part of its edge lies on the folding line.) Next, draw a half of a heart along the same edge. Finally, draw a half of a cat, with a tail, below the heart shapes. See Photo 3.

Cut and unfold. See Photo 4.

Photo 3

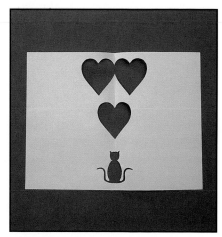
Photo 4

Note that your whole heart pattern resulted in two, linked, whole images—mirror images of one another. The half pattern produced a single whole. But the asymmetrical half pattern of the cat produced a pet you might not want to keep! To cut a shape that is not entirely symmetrical, first cut the symmetrical section (the cat's body), then unfold and cut the asymmetrical portion (the cat's tail) from the flat paper.

Learning the basic concepts involved in single-folded patterns will help to lessen the confusion that might result when you approach multi-folded patterns.

Double Folds

Paper can be folded more than once. The more folds you make, the more repetitions will appear in your pattern. Double folds can be made in at least two ways. The first method divides your paper into four quadrants.

Take a piece of paper and fold it in half. Now fold it in half again. See Photo 5.

Draw two half hearts, one on each fold line and cut out the one on the solid fold line. See Photo 6.

Photo 7 shows the unfolded paper. Your one half heart (on the solid fold line) has multiplied four times to give you two whole hearts. Note their positions on the paper.

What would have happened if you'd cut out the half heart on the other folded edge? Refold your paper and try it. See Photo 8.

As you can see in Photo 9, you've created another two hearts.

Now refold once again and cut a half heart on one of the unfolded edges, as shown in Photo 10.

Unfold the paper. Should we call Photo 11 a half-hearted effort? You can create lovely designs by using these unfolded edges, but don't expect to get whole images from the half images that you cut there!

Refold the paper and eliminate the half heart on the unfolded edge by creating a pretty, scalloped pattern instead. See Photo 12.

Unfold. Photo 13 shows a definite improvement.

The second double-folding method can be used to create patterns that extend along a horizontal line. Pennsylvania German housewives lined their

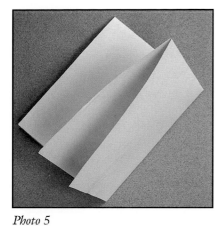

Photo 5

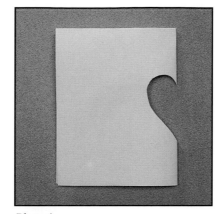

Photo 6

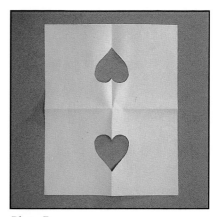

Photo 7

Photo 8

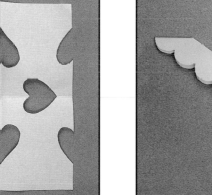

Photo 9

Photo 10

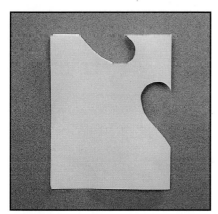

Photo 11

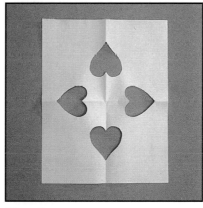

Photo 12

Photo 13

shelves with newspapers cut in this fashion; the decoratively cut edges of these cuttings hung below the shelves. Once you understand this folding technique, it's easy to make long chains and garlands too. Just be sure to draw your patterns in the direction that the chain will hang or drape. Use clear tape to hold a series of completed cuttings together.

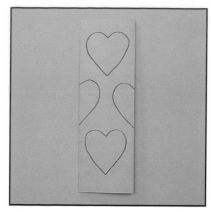

Photo 14

Photo 15

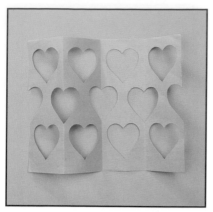

Photo 16

Photo 17

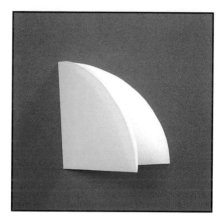

Photo 18

Photo 19

Photo 20

Fold your paper twice in the same direction. Draw two half-patterns on the folded edges and two complete patterns in the center. (You can also make an accordion-style fold.) See Photo 14.

Cut along the pattern lines, as shown in Photo 15.

Unfold. Note that the designs (shown in Photo 16) stretch along a horizontal line from one end of the paper to the other.

Be careful not to cut any lines that extend from one fold line to the opposite fold line; you'll find that your paper falls into two pieces if you do!

To make a circular, double-folded cutting, begin by marking a circle on your paper with a compass. Cut the circle out. See Photo 17.

Fold the circle in half once and then fold it in half again, as shown in Photo 18.

Draw patterns on both folded edges and in the center. Cut them out, as shown in Photo 19.

Unfold the circle. Notice where the cuts appear on Photo 20. Note too that when you cut away the folded circle's point, your finished piece will have a space in its center.

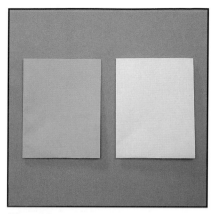

Photo 21

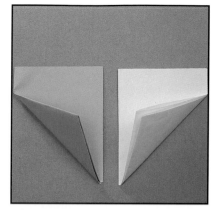

Photo 22

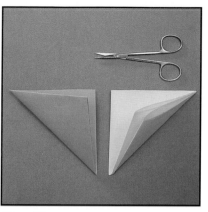

Photo 23

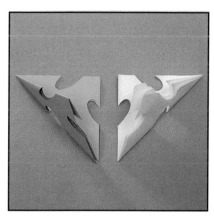

Photo 24

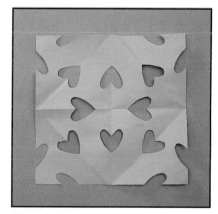

Photo 25

Photo 26

Triple Folds

Ready for more?

There are two common ways to create triple folds. Start with two pieces of paper. Fold each in half and then in half again. Place both folded papers in front of you with the last folds running along the right and the first folds running along the bottom, as shown in Photo 21.

Fold one piece by lifting the lower, left-hand corner until it reaches the right edge. Fold the other by lifting the lower, right-hand corner until it reaches the left edge. See Photo 22.

Cut off the excess paper on both pieces to form two triangles, as shown in Photo 23.

Though the two resulting triangles look deceptively alike, they are very different. The first will leave you with some unfolded edges on two of the triangle's sides. The second will leave only one of the triangle's sides unfolded.

A simple experiment will illustrate why these differences are significant. Draw half heart patterns on all three sides of each triangle, making sure that all the hearts are cut in the same direction. Cut all the patterns out, as shown in Photo 24.

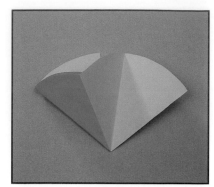

Photo 27

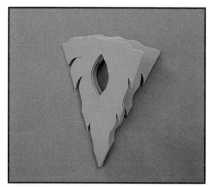

Photo 28

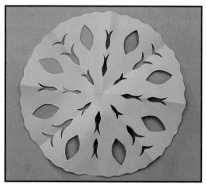

Photo 29

Photo 30

Now unfold the two cut sheets. Note the placement of the hearts on each cutting in Photos 25 and 26.

When you design triple-folded or multiple-folded patterns of your own, always cut them on scrap paper first.

Triple folding a circle results in a pie-shaped wedge. Lovely lace-like doilies can be fashioned from circular triple-folded paper. Begin by drawing a circle—with your compass—on a piece of paper. Cut the circle out. Fold it in half, in half again, and in half one last time. See Photo 27.

Cut any simple pattern on both edges and in the center. Add a border by cutting on the arc of the wedge. See Photo 28.

Unfold, as shown in Photo 29.

Multiple Folds

Folding frenzies won't damage your health, aren't addictive, and needn't be expensive. In fact, they're downright fun. Keep in mind, however, that cutting with precision through many layers of thick paper can be awfully difficult. Using thin paper for multiple folds cuts down on frustration!

One of the most common variations on multiple folding is the pie-shaped multiple fold on a circle. With a compass, draw a circle on a thin piece of paper and cut the circle out. Fold as you did for the triple fold but add a fourth fold. If you unfold the paper now, you'll see that you've divided the paper into sixteen sections.

Refold the circle. Then draw and cut at least one pattern in the center of the wedge. Draw and cut several patterns on the long, folded edges next. Unfold. The patterns you cut from the center (like the teardrop shapes in Photo 30) have repeated themselves sixteen times, as have the whole patterns cut on the folded edges.

Any half designs have also repeated themselves sixteen times, but because they were drawn and cut as halves, they now appear as eight wholes.

If you cut along the curved surface of the wedge, your circle will have patterns cut into and around its circumference.

Some intricate papercuttings are made by folding the paper several different ways. The artist will cut part of the pattern on a single fold, another part on a double-fold, and yet another on the unfolded sheet. Combining folding techniques can result in fascinating designs.

Circular Designs on Folded Squares or Rectangles

Creating circular designs on square or rectangular pieces of paper is easy; just cut patterns along an imaginary (or drawn) arc on the top fold. With this technique, it's easy to make rectangular place mats to complement your china plates.

Fold a square or rectangle of paper in half and then in half again. Place the paper in front of you with the last fold at the right and the first fold at the bottom. Lift the left-hand corner towards the right edge and fold when the two edges meet. If you like, add another, pie-shaped fold by lifting the edge at your left to meet the edge at the right again. With your compass point at the corner where all the points meet, draw an arc from one folded side to the other, as shown in Photo 31.

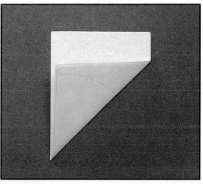

Photo 31

Draw and cut patterns along that line. See Photo 32.

When you unfold the paper, you'll find that the cut portions form a concentric circle, as shown in Photo 33.

No-Fold Patterns

Not all cuts are made on folded paper. Some papercuttings are assembled by layering small pieces of cut paper—one on top of another—into lovely collages. Traditional Polish cut work is often made in this fashion. Others are first folded and cut, and then unfolded and cut again to include asymmetrical design elements.

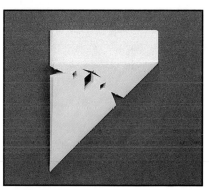

Photo 32

Now, sweep aside the small mountain of scraps on your table and relax! Though you may not believe it, as you practice folding, intuition will begin to take over. Until that magic moment, just rely on the project instructions in this book. They've been written to help you bridge the gap between logic and inspiration! And when you're ready to create and cut your own patterns, practice each one on scrap paper before you begin.

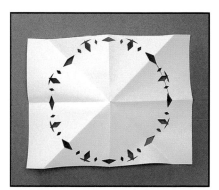

Photo 33

Peacock

18" (45.7 cm) x 18" (45.7 cm)

© 1989, Elżbieta Kaleta

Polish gwiazda (or star) design in the Lowicz style.

PRESSING OUT THE FOLDS

Unless you're making a three-dimensional ornament, you'll need to press out the crease marks from your folded cut work. Once you've finished cutting, and before you paint or embellish your paper, place the cut piece inside the pages of a heavy book. Leave it for a day or two to erase the creases. If you're in a rush, cut paper can also be ironed with a warm, dry iron. If your cut piece is painted, be sure to lay clean pieces of white paper under and on top of the cutting before you iron it. You wouldn't want any stray paint on your ironing board or iron.

TRANSFERRING PATTERNS

You'll have less difficulty finding patterns than you will resisting the overwhelming urge to cut them straight from the pages on which they're printed. (Patterns are available at craft stores, in books, and through mail-order sources.) Though you may itch to begin cutting right away, there are several disadvantages to doing so. First, the pattern may not be printed on paper that you like. Second, if the pattern is in a book, you'll have to tear the page out. Third, if you cut an asymmetrical pattern, your finished cutting will be reversed; whenever you cut a pattern, you always flip the finished piece over so that any remnants of pattern lines won't show. Finally, if you give the cutting away or frame it and then want to make another cutting based on the same pattern, you'll need to retrieve the original cutting (or take it out of its frame) in order to copy it. For all these reasons, your very first step should be to make at least one copy of any pattern you like before you cut it.

Leaving your cut work between the pages of a heavy book will press out unsightly wrinkles.

Graphite and transfer papers are available at craft and sewing supply stores.

Whether the original pattern is on a detachable sheet, on the page of a book, or is simply a finished cutting, you'll need to make sure that you have one copy to keep for future use and one to use in cutting. Keep in mind as you do this that patterns for folded cuttings are often displayed as a single segment of the total design. These partial patterns represent the cutting lines that will appear on the uppermost, visible portion of your folded paper. If you see a wedge-shaped pattern, for instance, you can be fairly certain that your cutting paper will be circular and folded several times. Transfer the partial pattern to one segment of your cutting paper and then fold and cut through all the paper layers simultaneously.

Copies can be made in several ways, but the easiest method is to head straight for your local photocopy shop and let the photocopy machine do the job for you. Make at least one copy the same size as the original.

If you'd like to copy a finished piece, but you don't have a pattern for it, you can use a photocopy machine to create one. Place the cutting on the copy machine's screen. If the cutting is white, place a piece of dark paper on its top surface before copying.

Another copying method is tracing. To do this, just attach a thin sheet of tracing paper securely to the original pattern with paper clips, staples, or tape. (Be sure to use very thin, transparent tracing paper.) Trace the pattern lines with a fine-lined, black-tipped pen or with a soft, sharp pencil that makes dark lines.

Transferring your traced or copied pattern to cutting paper can be done in a number of different ways. Each method works better in some situations than in others. Asymmetrical patterns, for instance, are tricky. Why? Take this hypothetical example. Imagine a bird design. The bird is looking toward the left side of the pattern sheet. If you trace that bird pattern, cut it, and then flip your finished cutting over so that any remaining pattern lines won't show, the bird will now be looking toward the right! No matter which method you use to transfer them, asymmetrical patterns always need to be reversed onto your cutting paper.

Once you've selected a pattern, just refer to the transferring methods described below and choose the most appropriate one.

Method One: Tracing a symmetrical pattern onto cutting paper

Fold the cutting paper as many times as the pattern calls for. Be sure to make sharp creases as you fold. Then unfold and place the sheet on top of the pattern, matching the crease lines with the pattern's marked fold lines. (The broken lines on patterns in this book always designate fold lines.) To keep the two sheets from shifting, use paper clips or staples to fasten them together. (Be sure not to staple through any areas that will show in your finished cutting.) Trace the pattern with a soft, sharp pencil.

When you're finished, refold the cutting paper so that the traced lines face up, and secure the folds with tape so that they won't slip as you cut through them.

If your cutting paper is too thick to see through, you'll need to place both sheets of paper over a light source, so that the lines are illuminated. You can purchase or build a light box, but it's just as effective to hold your papers over a brightly-lit window or glass door. Use your non-drawing hand to hold the papers in place as you trace.

If both your cutting paper and pattern paper are fairly transparent, you

My Spring Song
19" (48.3 cm) x 19" (48.3 cm)
© 1992, Sharon Schaich
Intricately cut and layered scherenschnitte

can also use this basic technique to trace an asymmetrical pattern onto cutting paper. Just be sure to flip your pattern upside-down before covering it with the cutting paper so that the pattern you trace onto the cutting paper will be a mirror image of the original.

Method Two: Photocopying a symmetrical pattern directly onto cutting paper

This technique will work only if the photocopy machine you plan to use will accept both your pattern and your cutting paper. Position your pattern face-down on the machine's screen and feed your cutting paper into the machine.

Note that this method will work only with symmetrical patterns. See Method Five for directions on photocopying asymmetrical patterns.

Method Three: Cutting a symmetrical pattern without transferring

You can avoid transferring altogether by cutting through your pattern and paper simultaneously. Fasten the two sheets together with paper clips, tape, or staples, and cut along the lines on the pattern through the cutting paper below.

Method Four: Transferring symmetrical patterns with graphite paper

Graphite paper is similar to carbon paper, but it doesn't leave unsightly smudges. Look for it at art supply and craft stores. Center a sheet of graphite paper on top of the cutting paper. Place the pattern copy on top of the graphite paper and fasten all three sheets together with paper clips, staples, or tape. With a sharp pencil, carefully trace over the pattern lines to transfer the pattern to the cutting paper.

Method Five: Photocopying asymmetrical patterns onto cutting paper

The finished side of all papercuttings is the non-cutting side. For this reason, asymmetrical patterns must always be transferred to cutting paper in reverse. There is a simple way to do this, but it will only work if you have access to a photocopy machine that will accept both your pattern and the cutting paper.

First, trace your original pattern onto very thin tracing paper. Next, take the traced pattern and your cutting paper to a photocopy shop. Place your cutting paper in the paper-feed bin. Then, instead of placing your traced pattern face down on the machine's screen (as you would do if you were making a normal copy), place it face up, with the penciled tracing lines facing you. The machine will copy that reversed image onto your cutting paper. Once you've cut that mirror image from your paper and have flipped the finished cutting over, the image you see will be exactly the one shown in your original pattern.

Method Six: Cutting asymmetrical patterns without transferring

This method is similar to Method Three but because you will need to reverse your pattern before cutting it, you must either use a reversed, photocopied pattern or a traced one. If you don't have a reversed photocopy, trace the original pattern onto very thin, transparent tracing paper. Flip the tracing upside-down and fasten it to your cutting paper with paper clips, staples, or tape. You'll be able to see the pattern lines through the tracing paper's surface. Just cut along these lines, through both the tracing paper and your cutting paper. Discard the damaged tracing when you're through.

Method Seven: Transferring asymmetrical patterns with graphite paper

This method is similar to Method Four, but because you're working with an asymmetrical pattern, one variation is necessary. You'll first need to trace your pattern onto very thin tracing paper and then, just as in Method Four, lay a piece of graphite paper on top of your cutting paper. Next, however, instead of placing the traced pattern on the graphite paper right side up, flip the tracing upside-down first. Fasten all three sheets securely with paper clips, staples, or tape. Retrace the pattern lines. As you do this, a mirror image of the original pattern will be transferred to the cutting paper.

ENLARGING AND REDUCING PATTERN SIZES

If you'd like to make a complex pattern easier to cut, just enlarge it so that all those twists and turns are magnified. Or challenge yourself by reducing the original pattern in size.

Photocopy machines can usually do this job for you, but if you don't have access to one, you can use a grid technique to enlarge and reduce by hand. This method does take a bit of time—and a bit of drawing skill—but works well even for people who don't think of themselves as artists.

First, using a pencil, draw a grid of equal-sized boxes over a copy of the pattern. Then, on your cutting paper, draw another grid composed of larger (or smaller, if you want to reduce), equal-sized boxes. Be sure that there as many boxes in this grid as there were in the original grid. For example, if you drew a 12-box by 12-box grid over your pattern, make sure that the grid on your cutting paper is 12 boxes by 12 boxes too.

Then draw the contents of each box on your original onto the similarly placed box on your cutting paper. Use the edges of the boxes as guides.

If a square on the pattern encompasses one half of a heart, for instance, draw a half heart in exactly the same position in the larger (or smaller) box of your grid. The grid just helps you to place your larger heart in the correct position on the cutting paper.

You can simplify this process considerably by finding and purchasing commercial graph paper with boxes printed exactly as large as you want. Various sizes of printed grids are available.

DESIGNING PATTERNS

Designing patterns isn't difficult, but choosing a way to begin can be! There are almost as many techniques for creating patterns as there are people to cut them. Some skilled papercutters work without any patterns at all; the images that live in their imaginations are transferred to paper as they cut. Others make sketches—hundreds of them—before a final pattern emerges. Still others modify traditional patterns to give expression to unique perspectives.

If you're new to design, one easy way to begin is with an actual object that you'd like to portray (or a photograph of it). In the illustration to the left, the artist has started by setting a lovely rose on a table where he can observe

it closely. He has deliberately chosen to look at it in a particular way, envisioning not only the petals but the spaces between each petal as well. Starting with the center of the flower, he has sketched the seven small shapes there. Next, he has shifted to petals further from the flower's center. Gradually, he's added more petal shapes until the entire flower has become a complete rose pattern.

When you try this technique yourself, remember that each shape you sketch will eventually be cut out. Your goal, therefore, is to sketch only the defining features of any object—the parts that really stand out.

You can also use needlework and quilting patterns as a source of inspiration. The very first paper cut-outs probably originated as a way of transferring embroidery patterns to material. Patterns were first drawn and cut on folded paper, and the cut paper was then pinned to material. Try reversing this technique; just trace or draw a design from a section of embroidered material or from a quilt. Many such designs reflect the symmetry of their folded, cut paper origins. Look closely at the pattern on the material, and your eye will quickly catch the pattern from which it was born.

ABOVE Untitled

P.G. Meppelink

If you have trouble originating patterns, search for symmetry in your surroundings.

OPPOSITE PAGE, BOTTOM
Embroidery patterns offer inspirations to designers.

If you find yourself facing a brick wall—totally uninspired—don't bang your head up against it; look at it instead! See the bricks as spaces and the mortar as connecting lines of paper. You'll find that both the natural world (the spreading branches of a tree, the ripples on a lake, the leaves on a stem) and the objects we've built within it (the grillwork on a gate, the windows in a tall building, designs on blanket chests and on tin and iron work) often carry within them the two elements most crucial to papercut designs: contrast and symmetry. The trick lies in learning to slow down long enough to really observe your surroundings—to look closely at light and shadow, at patterns, at shapes, and at sizes.

In some countries, each face of a mountain has a different name. People living to the west of the mountain call it by one name; people living to the east—because they have an entirely different view of its face—call it by another. Copying other people's papercut designs can provide lots of needed cutting practice and may even teach you some elements of design, but it won't teach you to name your own face of the mountain. When you copy someone else's designs, you won't learn to develop your own, unique perspective.

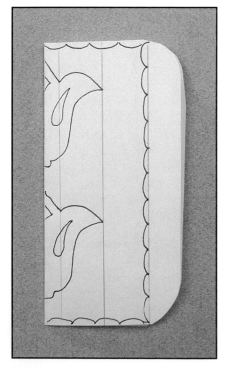

Guide lines serve as reference points when you sketch and cut.

Before you draw or cut a design on your paper, draw some parallel guide lines with a pencil. If, for instance, you plan to cut a flower pattern along a fold line, draw a vertical line parallel to the fold to indicate how far the tip of each petal should extend from the fold line itself. By using this line as a reference point, the petals you cut will all extend equally far from the fold line.

STAINING

As they age, some papers acquire a lovely, light-brown cast. Fortunately, you don't need to age along with them while you wait for this effect. As disreputable antique dealers already know, an antique look can be created artificially by applying tea or coffee. Parchment in an antique gold color is available commercially, but staining your own paper is inexpensive and fun.

You can stain paper either before or after you've cut it. If you stain after cutting, be sure that your hands are clean while you cut. Fingerprints will show up once the stain has been applied.

First, iron all wrinkles from your unfolded cut work with a warm iron. Then make a mixture of coffee and water and let it cool to room temperature. Place your cutting (display side up) on a large piece of waxed paper. Dip a small sponge (a cosmetic sponge is ideal for this purpose) into the coffee

mixture and carefully dab the cutting with the damp sponge until the cutting is saturated.

Wring the sponge dry and use it to clean up excess coffee from the waxed paper and cutting. Your finished piece will wrinkle and curl if it sits in unabsorbed liquid. Leave the cutting on the waxed paper, in a warm, shaded place, until it has dried thoroughly and then gently peel it off. Don't let the drying room get too warm; excessive heat will damage the paper. After the paper is dry, you may need to iron it again in order to remove wrinkles.

Some areas of your cutting may absorb more or less stain than others. This is a natural (and unavoidable) result of irregularities in many papers, so if your dried project looks slightly streaked or spotted, don't blame yourself—just enjoy the interesting and always unique results. Wrinkles, too, can be attractive. Leave a few to accentuate the paper's aged look.

Tea and coffee make excellent staining solutions.

ABOVE Painted Cows

Designed, cut, and painted by
Sandra Gilpin

RIGHT *Use watercolor paints on*
paper cut-outs.

PAINTING

Painting adds a personal touch to any cutting; no two painted cuttings are ever exactly alike. Whether you're a watercolor artist already or have never picked up a brush before, you'll enjoy adding at least a dab of color here and there.

There are two ways to paint cut work. The first is to paint and add detail lines before you cut. Transfer your pattern to parchment or calligraphy paper or to any paper that you know will accept paint well. If you want to include inked detail lines in the finished piece, use a fine-lined, felt-tipped waterproof marker instead of a pencil when you transfer the pattern. After you've painted, you'll cut along the outside of these inked lines, leaving the lines themselves for emphasis. The second method is to press and paint your cutting after it's completed.

The advantage to painting first is that you can cut away excess paint; your mistakes will disappear! But if you like, you can also paint the paper once each shape is clearly defined by the cut areas around it.

Believe it or not, the pattern offered here is based on the border design of a contemporary birth announcement. The proud parents—a dairy farmer and his wife—commissioned the artist to create a papercut announcement for the birth of their son. The finished cutting, modeled on those so carefully cut by Pennsylvania Germans years ago, includes the child's name, his date of birth, and the border from which this segment is derived.

What you'll need

    One 9" (22.9 cm) x 12" (30.5 cm) sheet of parchment or calligraphy paper, white or light tan

    Water color paints: raw umber, Prussian blue, yellow ochre, vermillion, green earth, Vandyke brown.

    #2 water color artist's brush

    Craft knife, #11 blade, and a cutting surface

    Scissors

    Pencil

    Black, waterproof, extra-fine, felt-tipped marker

    Masking tape

    White glue

    Dark-colored mat board for mounting

God's Promise

13" (33 cm) x 13" (33cm)

© *1991, Sandra Gilpin*

Appearances to the contrary, the cow design is cut from a flat—not a folded—sheet. Transfer the pattern from the photograph on page 48 by tracing all lines except the cows' spots with a fine-lined, black, waterproof marker. (Use a pencil to trace the spots.) The black lines will serve as both cutting lines and as details in the finished piece. You'll eventually cut around the outside edges of them, leaving the lines themselves to add detail.

Mix your watercolors, testing each one on scrap paper as you do. For an antique look, add a very small amount of raw umber to every color that you use and use a limited number of colors. Dip your brush into water, then into paint, and then apply the paint to the project. Be careful not to get your brush too wet, or the paper will ripple. If you'd like to run the edges of painted areas together, just paint one area and then paint the adjacent area before the first has dried.

Paint from the top of your cutting toward its bottom, leaving the solid borders until last. Once the painting is completely dry, press it on the wrong side with a warm, dry iron on a firm surface. You can add lettering to painted cuttings in a number of different ways. Using transfers and filling in the letters with India ink is probably the easiest.

ABOVE *You'll need glue if you plan to mount your cut work.*

LEFT *Add calligraphy or other pen-and-ink lettering for a special touch.*

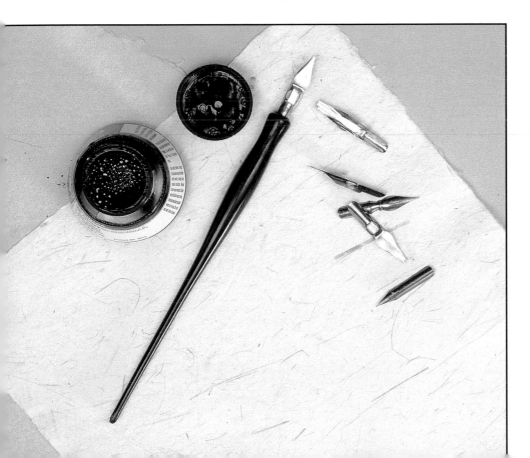

Use the felt-tipped marker to add additional details to the design (the cows' facial features, tree bark markings, etc.). Cut around the outside edge of the border first and then cut the small inside areas; work your way from the center to the outside edges of the pattern. A craft knife will work well on the fence and tree limbs (between the leaves). Manicure scissors are excellent for cutting the holes in the fence posts, the leaves, the cows' spots, and other curved areas. Cut the inside edge of the top border last.

GLUES

Finished cut work is often mounted on mat board or on paper that is thicker than the cutting paper. The best glues to purchase for this purpose are permanent spray adhesives recommended for use with paper, those that come in lipstick-shaped dispensers, wheat glues, and wallpaper pastes. White glue will work, but it tends to be too tacky and too easy to over apply.

White glues or wallpaper paste can also be used to repair minor tears. Apply a tiny drop with the point of a pin to bind two paper edges back together, or cut a small patch and glue it in place.

EMBELLISHMENTS

There's no reason why past tradition should dictate your own artistic expression. Though traditional cut work is rarely embellished with anything more than pinpricks, ink, or watercolors, nothing should stop you from adding imaginative extras to your own creations. A swirl of glitter or iridescent fabric paint, splashes of foil or tinsel, sewn buttons, small swatches of felt, or a strategically placed tassel or pompon can serve as your personal signature or playful statement (or both)! If calligraphy isn't among your skills, use stencil lettering instead.

You can also slice lines into your design without removing any paper. Graceful, curved cuts like these will highlight cut spaces.

MOUNTING AND FRAMING

If you'd like to frame your cutting, first iron any wrinkles out with a warm, dry iron. Then cut mat board, bristol board, or a similar backing to the size of your frame. Apply very small smears of glue or rubber cement to the corners and to select areas of the back of the cutting. Press the cutting into place on the board. You can also glue the cutting to thin cardboard and then mount the cardboard on fabric. Unless you add a mat border, the glass in the frame will hold the cutting flat against the mat board. If you add a

mat border to the mounted cutting, the glass won't hold the cutting in place. In this case, either mount the cutting with spray adhesive, which will affix the whole cutting to the board, or allow some sections of the cutting to float freely.

Sometimes it's best to glue fragile cuttings one section at a time. Mark the center sections of your mat board—the ones that will be covered by the finished piece—very lightly with a pencil. Glue the center of the cutting first by aligning it with the pencil marks. Then continue to glue small sections of the cutting in place, working from the glued center out toward the edges. Apply glue to each section by gently lifting that portion of the cutting and applying glue to its back.

Consider your frame size as you design your cutting. The finished cutting should be small enough to allow the mat board to provide a visual background and border.

As you start making the projects in the next section, you may need to refer back to these basic instructions once in awhile. That's to be expected. Before long, though, most of these elementary concepts will become second nature to you. In the meantime, you'll discover that the more you cut, the less frequently you'll need help. And the more you cut, the more you'll want to!

The Hunt

23" (58.4 cm) x 23" (58.4 cm)

© 1991, Elzbieta Kaleta

Single-folded pattern based on pottery designs

THE PROJECTS

Whether you're a beginner with scissors or an old hand at cutting, you'll find projects in this section to suit all skill levels and tastes. From framed cuttings to functional art, the patterns included range from traditional to contemporary and from simple to quite complex. Every project includes instructions, and most are also accompanied by helpful tips. These go one step beyond the directions given in the Basic Techniques section and will help you to overcome any cutting or assembly problems you might encounter.

As you select and cut these projects, don't be surprised to find yourself suddenly changing them. Inspiration has a wonderful way of striking when you least expect it. In fact, one of the joys of papercutting is that any pattern can be modified, and almost all designs can be used in a number of different ways. If you have access to a copy machine, for instance, you can enlarge or reduce pattern sizes to your heart's content. Nothing should prevent you from using a pattern for one project to make an entirely different project either. If you want to cut six bookmark patterns, fan them, and frame them—instead of sliding them into six best sellers—go ahead! If you have an overwhelming urge to sprinkle powdered sugar onto a cake through a Christmas ornament design, indulge that whim.

◆ 54

Before you start cutting, browse through the projects. Look for these symbols on each one:

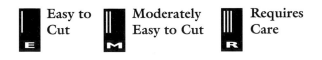

Easy to Cut   **Moderately Easy to Cut**   **Requires Care**

Keep in mind that dotted lines always indicate fold lines. Also remember that asymmetrical and symmetrical patterns require different pattern-transferring techniques. Once you've chosen a project, spend a couple of minutes reviewing any parts of the Basic Techniques section that apply. Then read the instructions for extra help. Experiment with newspaper before you start. Every cut you make will teach you something new, so think of that pile of scraps by your chair as lessons well learned.

OUT OF THE PAST:

TRADITIONAL PAPERCUTTING

Contemporary papercutting artists have inherited a wealth of inspiration from centuries past. Traditional symbols, styles, forms, and techniques from around the world often reappear in the best of today's cut art. The projects presented here illustrate the many ways in which modern papercut ters have selected from the best of their ancestors' experience.

PINEAPPLE

The pineapple motif is one of several that reappear frequently in Pennsylvania German scherenschnitte. Brighten your kitchen or breakfast nook with a finished and framed piece by mounting your cutting on mat board that matches the room's color scheme.

INSTRUCTIONS

This single-folded pattern is relatively easy to cut and will give you plenty of practice cutting both straight lines and curves. Once you've transferred the pattern, tape the edges of your folded paper together so that they won't slip while you're cutting.

Many of these project patterns have been reduced from actual size. Enlarge as necessary.

TIPS:

- Keep your scissors stationary and turn the paper as you cut.
- Remember to cut interior sections first.

ROOSTER

Roosters are popular subjects in wycinanki from all areas of Poland. This particular barnyard fowl is typical of the Lowicz regional style and is fashioned from cut layers of colored paper placed on a black background. His cheerful stance and brilliant colors make him look as if he might walk straight off the page!

Wycinanki are not impossibly difficult to make, but they do require some attention to detail as you transfer, cut, and layer the individual pieces. Read the instructions carefully before you begin the process of cutting and assembly.

PAPER

Fadeless, colored art paper is recommended for this project. Gift-wrapping paper and gummed-back art papers are good alternatives. You may choose any colors you like, but the traditional Lowicz style always calls for a black rooster and for light-colored papers in the layer closest to the black base.

READING THE PATTERN SYMBOLS

Note that the letters within the large rooster pattern match letters next to each smaller pattern shape. The letters within the larger pattern indicate where to glue the smaller patterns on the bird's body. The numbers following each letter on the smaller patterns indicate the number of layers included in each lettered portion. The wing pattern B-4, for instance, is made up of four paper layers. Those four layers will be glued, one on top of the other, to the portion of the rooster's body labelled with a B.

TRANSFERRING AND CUTTING PATTERNS

You'll find that transfer methods for this project are limited. (Refer to the Basic Techniques section for detailed instructions.) For the asymmetrical patterns, use Methods Six or Seven. For single-folded, symmetrical patterns, use Methods Three or Four. Notice that the patterns for layered sections are pictured as if they were stacked, one on top of another. You'll need to transfer these patterns one at a time, starting with the largest piece (designated by the exterior lines of each pattern set) and continuing on to the smaller pieces.

Keep in mind that most colored papers are colored on only one side. Patterns should be transferred to the white underside of these colored sheets, so that your scissors don't scratch the display side as they cut. For the same reason, colored paper should always be folded with the white side facing out. Don't forget to reverse each asymmetrical pattern piece as you transfer it to the cutting (or white) side of your paper.

GLUING

Wycinanki cut-outs are usually layered on poster board, mat board, or bristol board. Before gluing symmetrically cut pieces in place, the crease marks must be removed. Press each piece between the pages of a heavy book overnight or place each piece between two sheets of clean, white paper and then iron with a warm iron. A special gluing technique is used. Place each piece (face down) on a sheet of clear paper. Apply glue to its entire back, then turn it over and rest it gently on the mounting surface—don't press it down yet! Instead, cover the cut design with a fresh piece of white paper and press gently down

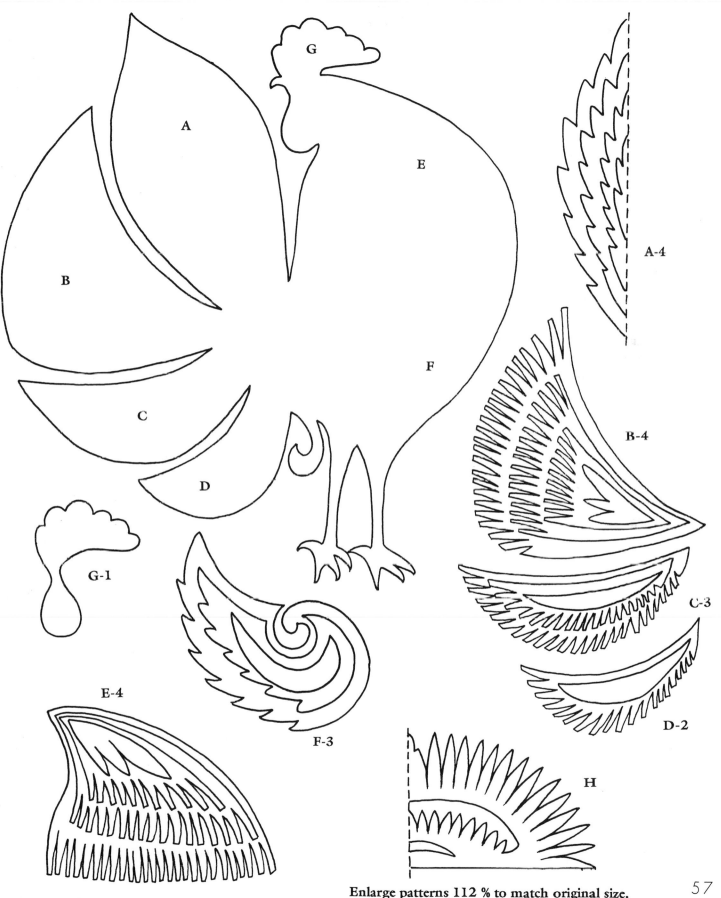

A

B

G

C

D

E

F

G-1

A-4

B-4

C-3

D-2

E-4

F-3

H

Enlarge patterns 112 % to match original size.

Rooster

© 1991, Elżbieta Kaleta

on that protective sheet. Lift and discard the protective paper.

Use white glue or a glue stick. If you're familiar with their somewhat messy application process, you may also use spray adhesives, but wear gloves, protect your eyes, and work in a well-ventilated area.

INSTRUCTIONS

First, transfer the large rooster shape (A-G) onto the white side of a piece of black paper. (Don't forget to reverse this asymmetrical pattern!) Cut the shape out. Next,

transfer and cut the foliage at the rooster's feet (H). This is cut from a single-folded piece of green paper. Glue the foliage (H) first. Then glue the black rooster (A-G) in place.

Cut out and glue the neck pieces (E-4). (Glue the largest shape first and follow with the smaller shapes.) Continue by cutting and gluing patterns B-4, C-3, D-2, F-3, and G-1. When you reach pattern A, note that each of the four pieces in it are cut from single-folded paper to produce symmetrical designs.

One pattern is not provided here—the rooster's beady little eye! Make this by creating a perfect circle of white paper with a one-hole punch. Draw a dot in the circle with a black marker and then glue the eye in place.

TIPS:

■ An extra pair of scissors, with curved blades instead of straight ones, will prove handy.
■ Don't use construction paper; it tends to fade quickly.
■ For added flair, cut one or two of the smallest patterns from metallic paper.

FEEDING TIME

In spite (or perhaps because) of its elaborate layout and time-consuming cutting requirements, the long, horizontal *kodra* design is a favorite among Polish papercutting artists. Every kodra combines both flat and folded cut-outs. These colorful papercuttings hang from the walls, exposed rafters, and beams of homes. They often include flowers, birds, or scenes based on everyday village life: work, holidays, ceremonies, and religious rituals.

Feeding Time depicts a farmer from the Lowicz region of Poland, clothed in a brightly-colored, traditional costume. He's obviously fond of his pet, whose house is even more elaborately decorated than the farmer's own dwelling!

INSTRUCTIONS

Before you begin, read the general instructions for the *Rooster* project on page 56. Similar construction techniques are used for this project. Use the photograph as a guide to color selections. It's important to note with this *kodra* that the small, layered patterns should be cut so that the individual pieces will stack evenly on top on one another. As an example, look at pattern M-2. The blue jacket piece in this two-piece design actually extends under the red trim piece. When you cut the blue section, you should cut around the exterior lines of pattern M-2.

Feeding Time
© 1991, Elżbieta Kaleta

Feeding Time - Kodra # 38   Elżbieta Kaleta 1992 ©

T

S-2

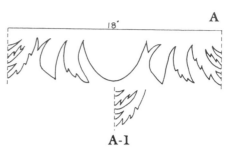

A-1

Using a ruler, measure a piece of green paper 18" (45.7 cm) long and 1 1/8" (2.8 cm) wide. Cut this piece out and fold it twice—horizontally—to create four layers of paper, each 4 1/2" (11.4 cm) long. Remember to fold the paper with its white side facing out. Transfer pattern A to the uppermost fold and cut it out. Then fold the paper one more time and transfer the smaller pattern A-1 to the arced area which will now lie at one edge. Cut this pattern out, unfold the strip, and press out the crease marks by letting the entire piece rest overnight under some heavy books or by ironing with a warm iron. Glue this grass border to your mounting board. If you like, decorate the grass with a long, narrow strip of colored paper.

Next, move to the tree (B-3). All three portions of this composite pattern are cut from single-folded paper. Transfer each pattern section to a different sheet and cut it out. Glue the cut pieces to the mounting board in sequence, using the photograph as a placement guide.

Cut and glue the house and its roof (C-2) next. No pattern is provided

for the narrow blue strips on the sides of the house; they are easily measured and cut without one.

The window pattern (D-3) consists of three pieces. The blue background is glued first, followed by the yellow frame. Then the green floral ornament above it is cut from single-folded paper and glued in place. The flower, for which no pattern is provided, is cut free-hand from flat paper.

The doghouse (E-3) is similarly decorated. Using the photograph as a guide, cut and glue the blue house first. Then cut and glue the black roof and black entrance. Note that you should cut these by following the exterior pattern lines for each; both should extend under the red trim. Next, cut and glue the red eaves and red entrance. As you can see from the pattern, these are all cut on flat sheets. Cut the two flower stems by cutting pattern G (twice) from two pieces of single-folded paper. Glue in place. Then cut and glue the greenery above the entrance (F-2) from two more pieces of single-folded paper. Finally, the flowers will need to be cut free-hand and glued in place.

Now that you've planted a tree and built the houses, you can try your hand at creating a man! Don't glue his body onto the mounting board until it has been completely constructed, however. As you assemble this section, check each cut piece for fit (and adjust it if necessary) by placing it in position before gluing it in place. Note that the trouser strips extend just slightly under the jacket and boots.

Cut the body, pattern H, first. Cut out the hair (I), the hat and band (J-2), and the white shirt (K). Check them for fit and glue them in place onto the body (H).

Next cut and glue the trousers (L)—with their decorative strips— to the body. Note that the orange trousers are a single piece. On the left leg, a wide black strip is first glued to the trousers, and a narrower yellow strip is glued on top of the black strip. On the right leg, a wide black strip lies on top of the leg, and a narrow green strip rests on top of the black strip's center. To the sides of the black strip rest a blue strip and a red strip; both are glued to the trouser leg.

J-2

I

K

P

O-2

R

**Enlarge patterns 200 %
to match original size.**

M-2

H

L

U

B-3

C-2

W-2

N

F-2

Gx2

D-3

E-3

Then cut and glue the black boots (U), the blue jacket and red trim (M), and the sleeves (N and O-2). Both the boots and the jacket will overlap the trousers slightly. The red strip of arm pattern O-2 is glued on top of the arm.

Cut and position (but don't glue) the bone (P) and the bowl (R)

between the man's fingers. Cut and then glue tiny pieces of red and black paper to the man's face to indicate a mouth, eyes, and eyebrows. Finally, glue the entire body to the mounting board.

Cut and glue the animals: the dog and ear (S-2), a pig (T), and two or more birds with tail feathers (W-2).

Don't forget the animals' eyes. Cut these free-hand from white paper, dot them with a black marker, and glue them in place.

TIP:

■ If you'd like to choose your own color scheme, experiment by layering shapes cut from scraps.

FLOWERS

Flowers can be found in traditional cut designs from Switzerland, Germany, the Netherlands, China, and Poland. Their universal appeal lies both in their beauty and in their suggestion of peace, happiness, and plenty. This design, a true challenge for the novice papercutter, is based on similar European scherenschnitte.

INSTRUCTIONS

Note first that the pattern does not include the finely-cut flower petals. Start by transferring the pattern to single-folded paper. Then cut the fine petal lines free-hand. If you wait to do this until you've cut the exterior flower lines, you'll find that your paper won't be stable enough to support itself as you make these delicate cuts. Though the skilled artist who designed and cut the original pattern used scissors, you may want to try a craft knife on this section of the pattern. Take your time. The flowers won't wilt if you set them aside for several days! When you've finished these, continue by cutting out the rest of the pattern.

TIP:

■ Note how the artist has accentuated the plain white of her cutting by mounting it on dark mat board and then surrounding it with contrasting red and complementary white mat boards. The simple wooden frame is not so ornate that it distracts the viewer from the lovely cutting.

STAR WITH BIRDS

The star is a recurrent motif in many Polish designs and can be cut from either circular or square paper. Folded varieties sometimes contain up to sixty-four repeats of a given pattern! In the Kurpie region (north of Warsaw), lacy stars are cut from a single color. Most are based on geometrical, multi-folded designs. Stars from the Lowicz region (west of Warsaw) shine with color. A symmetrical, one-piece, black design serves as the background for layered, colorful shapes—often peacocks or roosters surrounded by flowers and geo-metrical patterns.

Star with Birds

© 1991, Elżbieta Kaleta

INSTRUCTIONS

This traditional Lowicz star will entail cutting on both flat and single-folded paper. Read the general instructions given with the *Rooster* project on page 56 before starting. You may want to consider using a craft knife instead of scissors, in order to avoid the multiple punctures that would be necessary otherwise.

Begin by transferring the half-circle pattern (A-F) to the white side of a folded piece of black paper. Use paper clips to hold the two layers together or staple together sections that will eventually become waste. Cut and unfold. Press the crease marks out.

Before gluing this piece in place, lightly mark a center line on your board with a pencil. Turn the black star face down on a clean sheet of paper and apply glue along its central axis. Turn the star over and align it with the marked center line on the mounting board. Cover the star with a piece of clean, white paper and press down to affix. Remove the white paper.

Gently lift the right-hand side of the star and apply small amounts of glue to several sections. Carefully replace that side of the star onto the mounting board, cover with paper, and press down. Remove and discard the paper. Repeat with the left-hand side.

Transfer the five parts of each flower (A and B) to single-folded sheets of colored paper. Cut each pattern out and glue into place. Remember that the individual pieces are layered; they don't rest side-by-side.

In order to cut the bird patterns (C-2, D-3, E-4, and F-3) as mirror images of one another, cut each set from two sheets of paper that are clipped or stapled together face-to-face. For example, before cutting the large green outlines of the tail feathers (F), place two sheets of green paper together with the colored sides of each sheet facing each other. Clip or staple them together, transfer the pattern to

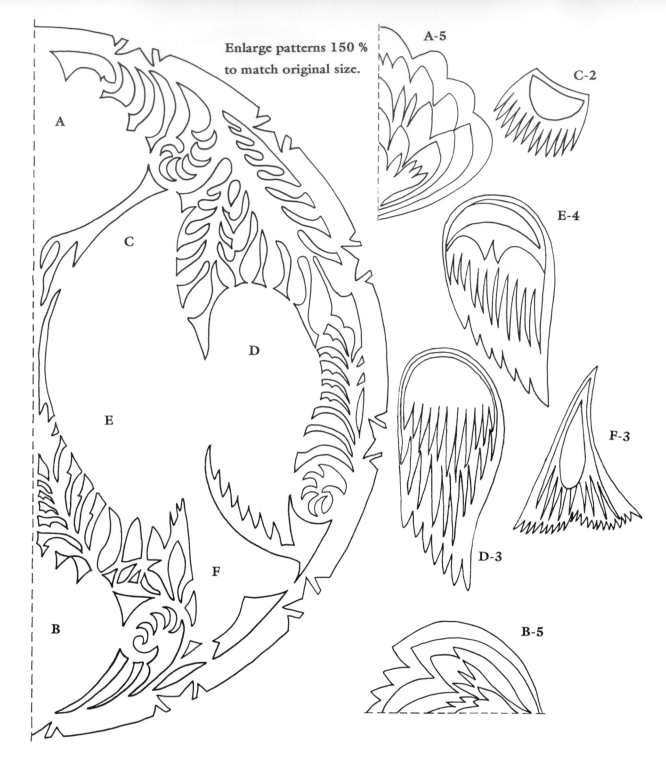

**Enlarge patterns 150 %
to match original size.**

A

A-5

C-2

C

E-4

D

E

F-3

F

D-3

B

B-5

the uppermost sheet, and cut.
You'll find that you end up with
two green tails, each slanted in
opposite directions.

When all the colored patterns have
been cut and glued in place, make

eyes for the birds and red dots for
the leaves by punching out circles
with a hole punch. If you have access
to a punch that will make smaller
holes, punch out two, smaller, black
circles for the white eyes and smaller,
red dots for the leaves. If you can't

find a hole-punch small enough, cut
these miniature dots by hand or
draw the dots with a marker.

TIP:

■ Disguise visible fold marks
with colorful strips of paper.

▌▌ DISTELFINK

Birds appear in papercuttings from around the world, often as symbols of life and hope. This charming *distelfink* design recurs in many Pennsylvania German cuttings as a symbol both of the Holy Spirit and of good luck. What better design to frame for a hall or entryway?

INSTRUCTIONS

The design (which has already been reversed for you) is a silhouette style and requires no folding. Simply transfer and cut. If you're using thin paper rather than parchment, try sandwiching your cutting paper between the pattern (on top) and a piece of typing paper or bond (underneath). Cut through all three pieces. Your cutting paper will be protected on both sides and will be much less likely to tear as you cut it.

TIP:

■ For an antique look, use antique gold parchment paper or stain your completed cutting with tea or coffee.

65 ◆

HAUS SEGEN

Visitors will always be glad they dropped by when they glimpse this traditional *haus segen* (house blessing) in your entryway. Haus segen were often painted quite ornately and embellished with *fraktur*, a German Gothic hand-lettering named for the broken or fractured appearance of its letters. The pineapple and distelfink motifs have been combined to suggest both abundance and peace.

INSTRUCTIONS

This design combines single-fold and no-fold cutting techniques. Because an asymmetrical section is included, the pattern must be reversed when it's transferred to cutting paper. If you've transferred the pattern correctly, the word "welcome" will appear backwards on the cutting side of your paper.

If you'd rather avoid cutting the very thin flower petals, just adapt the pattern so that each flower resembles a fluffy ball rather than a spiked one. If challenges appeal to you, though, start by cutting these intricate lines on your folded sheet. Then cut the other symmetrical portions. Finally, open the paper and cut the individual letters.

TIP:

■ You can use colored paper, but for a more traditional look, mount your cutting on mat board that will accentuate plain white or stained paper.

CHINESE CHRYSANTHEMUM

Each of the four major regions of China is represented by a flower. In the south, roses and peonies are popular. In northern China, where winters are dry and harsh, the two favorite flowers are ones which can withstand the inhospitable climate: the winter plum and the chrysanthemum. A symbol of strength and vitality, the chrysanthemum also represents the ability to overcome adversity. In the Chinese calendar, the chrysanthemum is the flower of the tenth month.

INSTRUCTIONS

The extremely fine lines of this magnificent pattern are cut with a craft knife on unfolded paper. If you feel insecure about cutting the fragile petals, just place your cutting paper between the pattern and another protective sheet before you start. You'll find that cutting through all three layers will prevent the petals from tearing.

TIP:

■ Try gluing only a few portions of this cutting to the mat board. The unglued portions will create distinctive shadow lines.

 CHINESE
HERON

Papercut herons have appeared
in Chinese cut work for centuries;
this pattern is based on an ancient
design. As in many Chinese patterns, cross-hatchings and angular
cuts manage to suggest a mood
as well as outline an object. This
graceful paper heron will look
best once it's framed.

INSTRUCTIONS

Stiff paper works well with this no-
fold pattern. The long, thin leg is
likely to bend or tear if you cut
from a very thin sheet.

CHINESE CARP

Though contemporary Chinese artists sometimes create original designs, older Chinese papercutting patterns are still passed along—unchanged—from generation to generation. In fact, skilled papercutters are proud of their ability to recreate inherited designs. Among the most popular of these patterns are those representing carp. The Chinese not only eat these fish but also consider carp as symbols of both determination and good luck.

One ancient Chinese fairy tale has it that a carp, in its migration upstream, leaped so high that it cleared the famous (and mythical) Dragon Gate. The fish is therefore thought to represent great leaps forward in good fortune. Paper cut-outs of carp are especially popular at the Chinese New Year.

INSTRUCTIONS

This design is cut from unfolded paper. Transfer the pattern and cut all interior portions first. If you plan to use delicate paper, sandwich your cutting paper between the pattern and another sheet and then cut through all three layers simultaneously. The exterior sheets will protect your fragile project paper as you cut.

TIP:

■ A Chinese papercutter would be very likely to cut this fish from red paper, as red is the Chinese color of good luck.

FROM THE SPIRIT:

HOLIDAYS AND CELEBRATIONS

In today's world of prefabricated plastic ornaments, handmade paper decorations can remind us that a celebration is only as meaningful as our own participation in it. Sure, it's easy to pick up a string of lights, a plastic pumpkin, or a gift tag at a department store. Anyone can do it—which may explain why holidays haven't been much fun in recent years. What's missing is you: your imagination, your participation, and your personal imprint on the season.

Why not bring yourself (and your whole family) back into the holidays you celebrate by making a few of your own decorations? Gather round the dining table, pass around the scissors, and share a few laughs. Don't rush, though. You don't have to make one hundred papercuttings this season. Just save the ones you do make and add a few more each year. Your children's children may be the proud recipients of your heirloom collection some day.

EASTER EGG DECORATIONS

Any child—or child at heart—will enjoy cutting and pasting these Easter egg ornaments—just as Polish children (and their parents) do. Simple colored cuttings look lovely on plain white or dyed eggs, but if playing with paint and glitter pleases you, embellish each decoration too. The small shapes can be glued onto boiled or hollow eggs. If the eggs are hollowed first, you can keep them indefinitely.

INSTRUCTIONS

The patterns illustrated include layered cuttings, single- and double-folded cuttings, and cuttings from unfolded paper. You can cut one piece at a time or stack sheets and cut out several, identical designs simultaneously. Be sure your eggs are at room temperature and are dry before you apply glue.

To hollow out an eggshell, make a small hole in one end of an uncooked egg with a large pin or small knitting needle. On the other end, make a slightly larger hole. Break the yolk by gently probing it with your needle. Hold the egg over the sink or a bowl and blow into the smaller hole until the contents are emptied from the egg. Rinse the shell out with cold water.

TIPS:

- Some decorations are easier to glue if you cut slits in their edges so that they can be bent to fit the contour of the egg.
- If you glue decorations onto hard-boiled eggs, don't eat the eggs unless you're sure that the glue isn't toxic.
- Finish cutting all your decorations before you start gluing, or you may find yourself better decorated than your eggs—glue has a mysterious way of creeping onto skin!

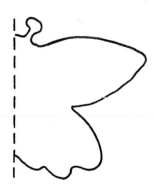

HALLOWEEN DECORATIONS

It's difficult to be appropriately frightened by patterns as easy to cut and to store, but who cares? Though the vampire bat and cat patterns may not scare you, they're sure to attract the more courageous of your neighborhood's treat seekers. Perch them on a window sill, hang them in a doorway, or send them as Halloween cards.

INSTRUCTIONS

Transfer either pattern to single-folded paper and then cut it out. You'll be folding back the bottom edge of the vampire pattern's border, so make it extra wide. Cut a piece of backing and glue the cutting to it by applying small amounts of glue to a few areas of the cut piece and pressing it in place. Note that the cats are backed by two pieces of paper, each a different color.

TIP:

■ If you don't have extremely sharp scissors, use a craft knife to cut the eyes and teeth on the bat.

CHAINS AND STREAMERS

Long rows of cuttings are perfect decorations for seasonal celebrations. Let Halloween trick-or-treaters know you're in business by hanging a strip of welcoming paper pumpkins in your window or wrapping one round the candy dish. Share Christmas preparations with your family by making papercut streamers for the tree. Celebrate a birthday by wrapping a cutting around a cake. The design possibilities for long papercuttings—ones that sway and stretch and dangle—are almost endless, but they're all based on a simple, horizontal (or accordion-style) folding technique.

INSTRUCTIONS

Fold cutting paper horizontally as many times as its thickness (and your wrist strength) will allow. If you'd like a really long banner, attach several completed papercuttings together with invisible tape. Vertical streamers can be tricky. Be sure to use a design that is without a top and a bottom—a circle, for example. If you try to cut birds to hang vertically, on horizontally folded paper, half of the poor creatures will be upside-down!

TIPS:

■ Mount these cuttings on strips of contrasting paper or hang them in front of a lit window at night.

■ Cut a streamer from waterproof acetate and let it sway from the ceiling of your veranda or porch.

GIFT RIBBONS

Wrapped gifts always look incomplete without ribbon, but why buy rolls when you can easily cut a design in paper instead? You'll have a lot more fun making these decorative strips than you would on a last-minute shopping spree, and you'll spend a lot less money too. In fact, the only disadvantage to these stunning papercut ribbons is that they're likely to be get more attention than the gifts themselves!

INSTRUCTIONS

First, cut a long strip of paper. Fold it twice—or more, if it's thin—horizontally. Unfold and transfer your pattern to one segment of the strip. Refold and cut.

TIPS:

■ For extra color, back the cut paper ribbon with a strip of colored paper.

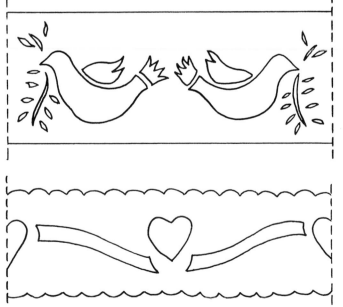

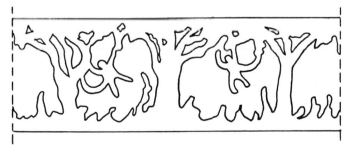

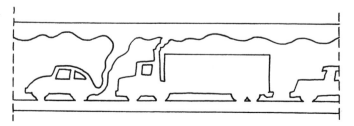

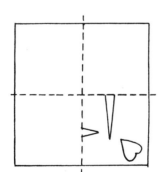

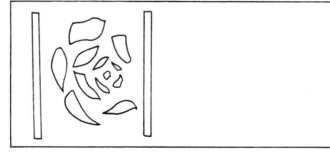

To
From

GIFT TAGS

Cut paper gift tags are gifts in themselves. They're fun to design, easy to cut, and quickly assembled too. The next time you wrap a present for someone you love, take ten minutes to add that special touch; all you need are scissors and a bit of paper.

INSTRUCTIONS

You can use almost any kind of paper for this project, though stiff papers work best for folded tags. The patterns offered here include unfolded, folded, and layered designs. You can fold your finished cuttings into miniature cards, string them on ribbon, or embellish them with paint and glitter. The possibilities for making unique tags are almost endless.

NO-FOLD PATTERNS

Transfer the entire pattern to a flat sheet of paper. (If you plan to fold your tag after it's cut so that the cut portion is on the front, leave an uncut section attached to serve as the tag's back.) For color contrast, either mount these tags directly on your wrapped gift or cut a piece of colored paper slightly smaller than the tag itself and glue it to the back of the tag.

FOLDED PATTERNS

Fold your paper, unfold it, transfer the pattern, refold, and cut. Unfold and mount on colored paper, on a folded piece of card stock or paper, or on the gift itself.

LAYERED PATTERNS
(No-Fold and Folded)

Cut patterns from separate sheets of paper and glue the smaller pieces to the larger ones.

TIPS:

- Use stencil patterns for perfect lettering or leave plenty of uncut space for writing.
- Glitter, paint, and ink all look lovely on tags.
- Fasten the tag to a gift by running a matching ribbon through a hole in the top of the tag; your one-hole punch will come in handy here.

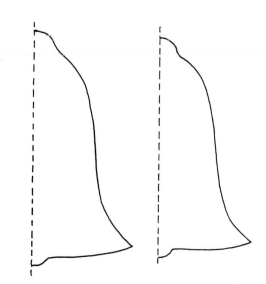

THREE-DIMENSIONAL CHRISTMAS CENTERPIECE

"Christbaum und Tischschmuck-schnitte" (Christmas tree and table decoration cuttings) are traditionally cut from plain white paper, but these economical decorations can be adapted (in size, design, and color) to suit both your interior decor and the occasion. Once they've been assembled, you can embellish them in any number of ways: with glitter, miniature paper ornaments, tinsel, writing, or tiny pieces of paper or felt. Because they're cut from fairly stiff paper, paper centerpieces will last for years. When they're not in use, just fold them flat and pack them between two pieces of cardboard.

This project gives festive voice to a popular Christmas carol. Each carefully cut row of figures—from the twelve drummers drumming at the bottom to the partridge in a pear tree at the top—is a perfect rendition of one line from "The Twelve Days of Christmas."

INSTRUCTIONS

You'll need four sheets of stiff paper (in any color) and a craft knife. Don't fold your paper before cutting it. Even though this tree design is based on a single-folded pattern, the thick paper is more easily cut when it's flat.

There are two patterns. One represents the top half of the tree, and the other represents the bottom. You will cut each pattern twice so that you have two tops and two bottoms with which to construct two complete trees.

Start with the top pattern by transferring it to stiff paper. Because both sides of your cut paper will show once the centerpiece is assembled, you'll want the pattern lines to be clear enough to see as you cut, but not so thick that they show when you're finished.

Then place a ruler along the dotted lines at the center (top and bottom) of the transferred pattern. With your craft knife, score a line from top to bottom of the center line, but don't let your knife go all the way through the paper. This line will become a clean, sharp fold line when the project is assembled.

Cut along the pattern lines with a craft knife. Work from top to bottom and from the center outward,

cutting the smallest details first. Perforate the paper with a large needle to create eyes.

Repeat these steps with the bottom pattern and then glue the top piece to the bottom piece by running a thin line of white glue along the shaded portion of the bottom piece. Spread the glue with your finger, press the top portion in place, and allow the glue to dry. Trim if necessary.

Repeat all these steps with the other set of top and bottom patterns.

When both pieces are dry, you may fasten them together in one of two ways. To sew them together, lay them directly on top of each other, with their scored lines touching. Rest a ruler along the vertical center line of the tree on top, and use a sharp pencil to make small dots at 1/4" (.6 cm) intervals from the top to the bottom of the tree. Making sure that both trees are aligned, punch a small hole at each dot with a push pin. Be sure that the holes extend through both trees.

Thread a needle, but don't tie a knot in your thread. Beginning at

The 12 Days of Christmas
© 1991, *Papercuttings by Alison*

You can also glue the two trees together, though this is more difficult to do. Bend each tree along the crease line until its two halves are at right angles. Apply a very small amount of glue along the crease line on both pieces and then press the two crease lines together gently. It's best to do this with the pieces standing up. If you try to glue them flat against each other, the center line may come unglued when you try to bend the tree later.

TIPS:

■ To simplify cutting this stiff paper, hold your knife with the blade facing you and slide the paper into it with your non-cutting hand. Twisting and turning the paper is much easier than twisting and turning the knife blade.

■ You can mount these cuttings by leaving an ample uncut portion at the bottom of each piece. Score these sections and—after joining the two trees—fold them back. Glue them to a piece of mat board so that the centerpiece will rest solidly on any flat surface.

the top, sew the two trees together with a running stitch, using the holes you've made as points of entrance for your needle. Leave plenty of thread at the starting point; you'll be making a knot with it once your needle returns to that position. Your needle should go in the first hole and come up through the next hole. When you reach the bottom, flip the trees over and sew back up along the other side. Make a small knot with the thread ends. Finally, fold back each tree along its crease line, so that the four quarters of the tree extend at right angles.

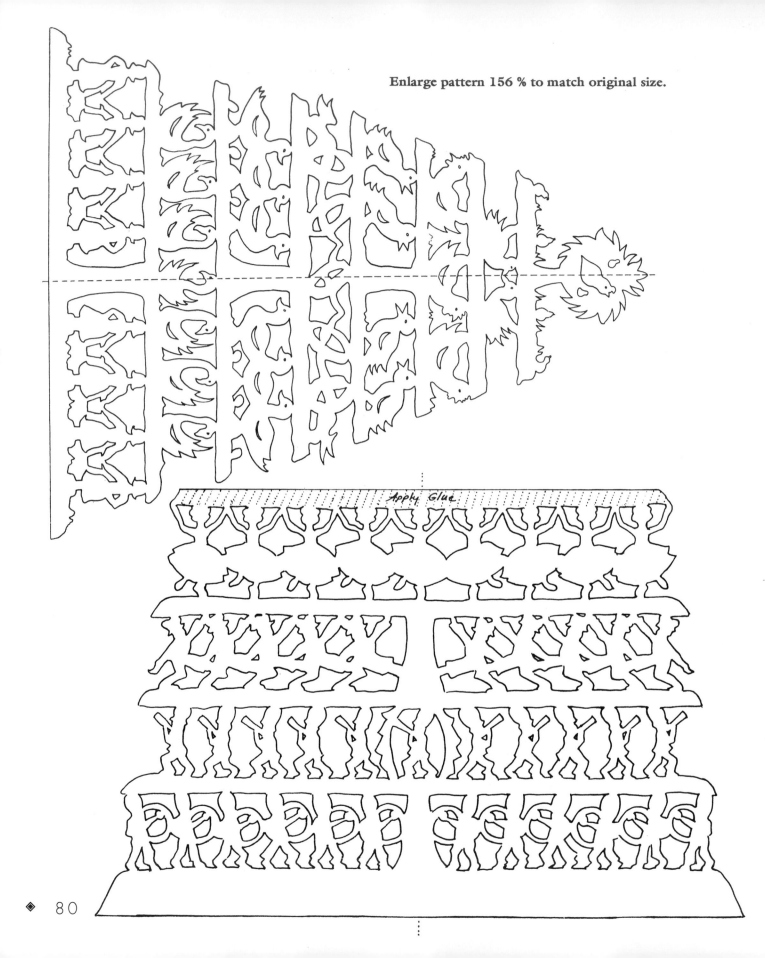

Enlarge pattern 156 % to match original size.

Apply Glue

CHRISTMAS TREE ORNAMENTS

Add to the festive spirit of any seasonal celebration with a few paper-cut ornaments. These are surprisingly easy to make, but even the simplest of papercuttings looks impressively ornate when it's transformed into a three-dimensional hanging ornament. Don't limit yourself to hanging these decorations on trees either. They look just as attractive attached with ribbons to gifts, dangling from doorways, and even hanging on houseplants!

INSTRUCTIONS

Hanging ornaments are made in much the same way as the *Christmas Centerpiece* project (see pages 78-79.) Note, however, that the stiff paper used to make a centerpiece requires no-fold cutting; ornaments can be made of more flexible paper and can be folded before they're cut. They won't need scoring either.

Select a pattern and transfer it to single-folded paper. Then cut the pattern out twice, so that you have two identical cuttings. (Don't worry about minor differences between the two; these won't show once the ornament is assembled.) If you're using thin paper, you can cut both patterns at one time.

You can also cut three identical patterns to create an ornament with six—instead of four—divisions.

Place one completed cutting on top of the other so that the cuts on both are aligned. Tape the edges of the cuttings together. Lay a ruler along the center line. With a pencil, make light marks at 1/4" (.6 cm) intervals. With a push pin, make a small hole at each mark.

Thread a needle, but don't knot it. Starting at the top, and using the pre-made holes, stitch the cut pieces together with a running stitch. Leave plenty of thread at the starting point. When you get to the bottom, flip the ornament over and stitch up the opposite side to the top. Make a loop by tying the remaining thread ends together. Bend the four segments of the sewn ornament so that each is at right angles to the next.

TIPS:
- Embellish your ornaments with glitter before stitching them together.
- Stiff paper ornaments with bent bottom edges will stand on flat surfaces.
- Store ornaments by folding them flat between two pieces of cardboard.

▐▌ PRINTED
▐▌ GREETING CARDS

Friends who receive your personally designed cards are likely to treasure them for a lifetime. Not only are these cards distinctive in appearance (a welcome relief from the commercial card patterns that we all know by heart), but they're reasonably inexpensive to make as well. A pair of scissors, cutting paper, card stationery and envelopes, and an accessible print shop are all you need.

INSTRUCTIONS

First, pay a visit to your local print shop. Ask to see their blank card stock. Many shops cut their own stock to standard card sizes, and you'll need to know what sizes are available to you. Explain that you'd like to have some cards printed; select a card size and a color for the ink itself.

Next, you'll need a papercutting—one to suit the card that you have in mind. The wonderful trick here is that your cutting doesn't have to be as small as your intended card. In fact, if you're a novice, cut a large, simple pattern. You'll photocopy your finished cutting, using the copy machine's reduc-

tion capabilities, and your simple—but smaller—cutting will look flatteringly complex!

Once you've cut your design, take the unframed, pressed papercutting to a photocopy shop. Make one, clear, black-and-white photocopy of your papercutting, reducing its size to fit your selected stationery.

Finally, take the photocopy to the print shop and tell the printer how many cards you want. The printer will take care of the rest!

83 ◆

TIPS:

■ The fewer cards you have printed, the higher the cost will be. If you only need a dozen cards, you might consider having them color-copied instead of printed. Your print or photocopy shop can help you decide which method to choose.

■ Individualize your printed cards by embellishing each one in a different way. Calligraphy, glitter, or paint will add a special touch to every finished piece.

HAND-CUT CARDS

Once in awhile, you'll want a very special card for a very special person. No store-bought or printed card will do. Nothing will convey your special feelings as well as an elegant, papercut card—a lovingly created, one-of-a-kind keepsake. These Christmas cards and the valentine may inspire you to try designs of your own. In the mean time, the patterns provided are certainly well worth the time they'll take to cut and assemble.

LEFT Holiday Wishes (Peace, Love, Noel, and Christmas Tree)

© 1992, Papercuttings by Alison

INSTRUCTIONS

Note that the asymmetrical pattern has already been reversed for you. The Christmas tree pattern, the house design, and the valentine are cut from single-folded paper. To make the *Noel* card, transfer the pattern and cut its symmetrical portions on a single fold. Then unfold your paper and cut the asymmetrical, center section.

Your finished cuttings can be assembled in a number of ways. Perhaps the simplest of these is to glue your cutting either to the inside (or front) of a stationery-weight, folded piece of paper or to a purchased card blank. Choose papers for your cutting and card that will complement each other in color. Then decide how large your card will be. If you want an envelope, check to be sure that one is available to match the selected card size. Make the cutting slightly smaller than the surface of the card to which it will be glued. The background border provided by the card material will serve as a visual frame.

Glue the finished cutting to the front or to one of the inside surfaces of the folded card.

Original cuttings can also be mounted before they're affixed to selected card materials. Make a backing out of complementary mat board or paper that is slightly larger than the papercutting but slightly smaller than the card surface. Mount the cutting on the backing, and then glue the backing to the card. An attractive color contrast can be created by using only two colors; the cutting and card are made from one color and the backing from another.

Eighteenth and nineteenth century liebesbriefe usually weren't mounted at all. For contemporary valentines of the same sort, use a fairly stiff paper, as they're likely to be admired (and handled) frequently!

You can also cut the card stock itself. Folded cards, with a cut front half and an uncut back portion are fairly easy to make. The selected paper or card is folded in such a way that only the front portion is cut. Contrast between cut and uncut halves can be provided by gluing a piece of colored paper to the back of the cut half, by painting the cut half, or by painting the back, uncut half to serve as a background.

TIPS:

■ Elaborate on any of these methods; they're certainly not the only ones possible! Let your imagination play with each variable: color, size, shape, folds, location of cuts, and mountings. You'll soon discover as many possibilities for card styles as you have deserving friends to receive them! And don't stop once the card is cut and glued. Push pin holes, glitter, sequins, written messages, collages made from cut paper or material—can transform a simple pattern and technique into a one-of-kind marvel.

■ Any of these cards will make a memorable, framed gift as well.

Enlarge pattern 126 %
to match original size.

FOR THE RECORD:

READING, WRITING, AND KEEPING TRACK

The human need to keep track of significant events, people, and objects in life is as old as man himself; cave paintings testify to our ancient need to record the significance of our lives. Today, computers keep up with what we own, what we owe, our birth dates and weddings and deaths, but before technology embraced the world we live in, cut paper art often served to proclaim and celebrate people's individual and collective histories.

To these two people, namely Hans Traphagen and his lawful wife Gudrun, nee Logeman, a daughter was born into the world by the name of

Heidi Gretchen

in the year of our Lord 1803, the 21st day of June, Lancaster County, in America, in the State of Pennsylvania

BIRTH ANNOUNCEMENT

During the eighteenth and nine-teenth centuries, Pennsylvania German and Dutch immigrants often embellished their documents with cut designs and fraktur. Birth, baptismal, and marriage certifi-cates—as well as wedding an-nouncements and other important papers—were lavishly cut. The intricacy of these cuttings and the unique styles of individual paper-cutters made illegal replication virtually impossible. Laced with symbolic images of hope, religious faith, and love, each cut paper certificate bore witness to the event for which it was created.

INSTRUCTIONS

If you'd like to frame your cut certificate, enlarge (or reduce) the border pattern to fit the frame. Transfer the pattern to double-folded paper and cut. (The white circle in the center of each pattern should be cut separately.) Mount the cut border on an appropriate backing. Write the words of the announcement on your cut circle of paper and then mount the circle in the center of the cut border. Calligraphy adds a special touch.

TIPS:

■ These patterns also make delightful frames for round photographs or paintings.

■ If you'd like to paint your cut border, you can either paint the completed, ironed cutting, or you can transfer the whole pattern to cutting paper (in-stead of just half of the pattern), paint it, and then fold and cut.

■ For an antique look, stain with coffee or tea before mounting.

Enlarge patterns 160 % to match original size.

■ BOOKPLATES

Bookplates originated many years ago, when books were so costly to produce that only the wealthiest of people—or the most addicted and frugal of readers—could afford to buy them. Each treasured book was labelled with the name of the person to whom it belonged. Rather than sign their books, however, proud owners wrote on small, exquisitely painted or cut pieces of paper and pasted these book-plates—as they were called—onto the books' inside cover or flyleaf.

Today, even though books are widely available, bookplates are still used to designate ownership and to add beauty to the books they adorn. Those of you who lend books frequently are likely to reap an additional benefit—your bookplates will serve as gentle reminders to friends who borrow from your library!

INSTRUCTIONS

The patterns illustrated here may be enlarged or reduced as needed. The asymmetrical pattern has already been reversed, so you won't need to flip it over. Any paper can be used, though antique parchment looks well on older books. Write the name on your pattern before you cut.

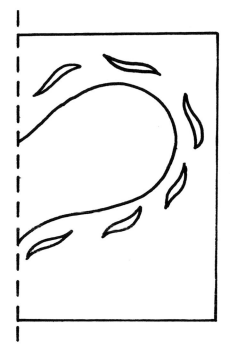

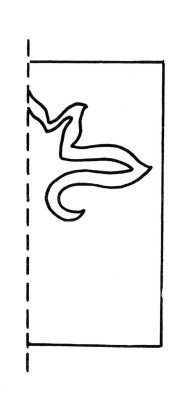

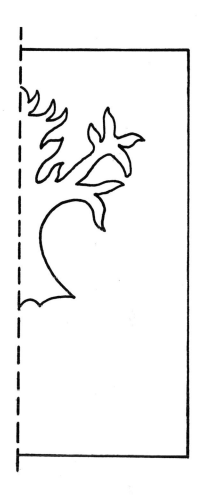

TIPS:

■ Add the Latin phrase *Ex Libris* (from the library of) in front of your name.

■ Calligraphy looks especially impressive on bookplates.

■ To provide color contrast, mount your bookplate on colored paper and then glue the mounting to the inside of the book.

■ If you plan to give a book as a gift, include a bookplate. Add the date and the occasion to the recipient's name.

BOOKMARKS

People who love to read are prone to two bad habits: bending down page corners and leaving open books face-down. The first habit leaves unattractive crease marks on pages, the second cracks a book's binding, and both can induce horrible guilt. Lighten your life—and preserve your library—by making a few cut paper bookmarks. These individualized markers are a delight to behold, make wonderful gifts, and will last indefinitely if you leave them in a book between bouts of reading.

INSTRUCTIONS

The asymmetrical patterns have already been reversed. Assemble the flower cutting (pictured to the right) by first gluing a piece of tissue to its back and by then gluing another piece of parchment to the back of the tissue. Punch a hole through the top center with a hole punch. Then loop and knot some embroidery thread through the hole. The sandwiched tissue provides color contrast, and the parchment back serves to stiffen the bookmark.

The leaf cutting is mounted on dark green paper. The single-folded heart pattern is first cut from parchment and then mounted on two, folded strips of colored paper.

When you attach these strips, be sure to apply glue to the delicate portions of the cuttings, or they'll soon become ragged. Be careful, though, not to apply too much; any excess will tend to stick to the book's pages.

TIPS:

■ Copy a picture of your favorite author. Then create and cut a pattern that leaves room for the picture in its center.

■ Personalize gift bookmarks by including the lucky recipient's name.

■ These patterns can also serve as calendar markers. Just cut a small version, punch a hole at the top, and tack the marker to any "red letter" day on your calendar.

PLACE CARDS

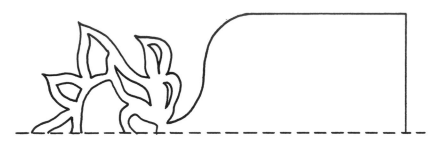

Whether you're entertaining at a formal dinner or planning a birthday party for your eight-year-old, place cards not only help to prevent party pandemonium when it comes time to seat everyone, but also add a personal touch to each setting. Cut designs to match the menu, the china, or the mood.

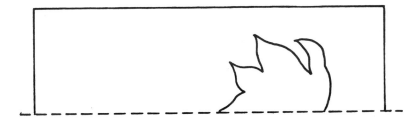

INSTRUCTIONS

Unless you plan to tuck your place cards into napkin rings or rest them flat on a plate, you'll need to stiffen them so that they'll stand up. Although all of the patterns pictured are cut from single-folded paper, each has been backed in a slightly different way. The star pattern was stiffened by gluing a thick piece of paper to its rectangular back. Another piece of antique parchment was then glued to the thick paper. Finally a small strip of parchment was cut, and folded in half, and its upper portion was glued to the back to act as a brace.

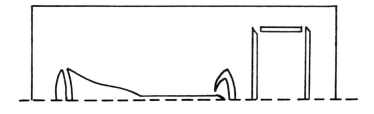

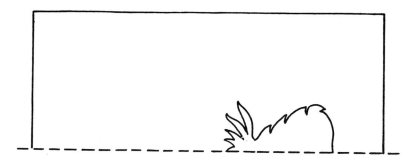

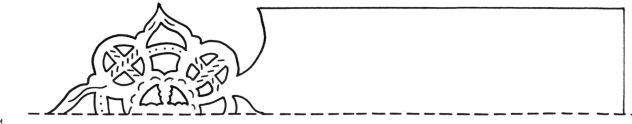

The wine glass place card was similarly stiffened, but colored tissue was used instead of thick paper. The pineapple and flower patterns don't need bracing; they rest on their folded backs. Both have contrasting paper glued behind their cut, front sections. The floral pattern (pictured in the napkin ring) was backed with thick paper and antique parchment. Note that its central box lines were cut after the backing was glued in place.

TIPS:

■ Paint or write the name of your guest before you glue a backing to your card.

■ Embellished or not, place cards make wonderful party favors.

■ You can also brace place cards by rolling the bottom edge with the blunt side of a scissors' blade.

IN THE HOME:

DECORATIONS

Not everyone can afford to commission family portraits or paintings to match their interior decor. The earliest papercutters certainly couldn't, but these pioneers knew that beauty was as accessible as the nearest pair of scissors and piece of paper. From brightly-colored Polish wycinanki to framed silhouettes, cut paper has satisfied a universal need for decoration since paper was first invented.

 JAR LINERS

Glass jars can be transformed from handy containers into decorative delights by lining or covering them with cuttings designed to complement their contents or your home's decor. Any mantel or shelf will benefit from a row of bright and cheerfully decorated jars. Try flower and herb designs for potpourri and pasta patterns for the macaroni!

INSTRUCTIONS

Measure the circumference of your jar. Cut a piece of paper to size and fold it twice, horizontally. Transfer the pattern, cut, and unfold. Iron out wrinkles and slip the cutting into the jar or glue it to the exterior. You can add a drop or two of non-toxic glue to hold the paper to the inside edges of the jar if its contents won't hold the papercutting in place.

TIPS:

■ Be sure not to cut out areas so large that the contents of the jar will slip between the cut areas and the glass when the cutting is inside.

■ Use a fairly stiff paper so that it won't be damaged by what's inside the jar.

■ Personalize a gift jar by including a cut or written message on the liner. Don't forget to add a cut paper gift tag too.

BORDERS

When treasured photographs and pictures are enhanced by cut paper borders, their best qualities are revealed. The photograph of the two brothers is a marvelous study in contrasts: the boys' different sizes, the silhouette effect of their shapes against the bright sky, and the reflected light against their dark clothing. These contrasts are complemented by the simple border that their mother designed and executed specifically for this photograph of her sons. Note, too, how well the framed pattern pictured here complements both its frame and the photograph in it. The antique parchment color blends superbly with both the child's hair and the wooden frame.

INSTRUCTIONS

First select a frame for your picture. The best frames are those that won't detract from the cut border, so avoid frames that are more ornate than your cutting pattern. Then enlarge or reduce the pattern to fit your frame and the picture in it. (Two of these patterns are cut from double-folded paper. The leaf pattern is a single-folded design.) Transfer the pattern, but before you cut the actual border, unfold your paper and check to see that the center section fits perfectly over the photograph and that the outside edges fit the frame.

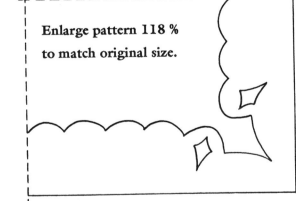

Enlarge pattern 118 % to match original size.

TIPS:

■ Mounted borders will last longer if they're framed under glass.

■ Oval border patterns are especially appropriate for portraits and silhouettes.

■ Cut paper borders look lovely around the glass in bookcases and cabinets, though you'll need to assemble them from several strips of cut paper.

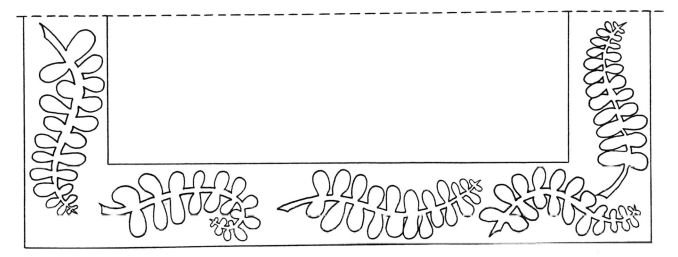

Enlarge pattern 123 % to match original size.

Enlarge pattern 123 %
to match original size.

99 ◆

SILHOUETTES

Silhouettes reached a peak of popularity during the late eighteenth and early nineteenth centuries. These cut profiles were an inexpensive but aesthetically pleasing alternative to portraiture. The best silhouette artists were those who were able to notice and portray their models' personalities. Notice that the simple lift of this subject's chin reveals her determination as clearly as might the word "stubborn" printed across her forehead!

Both the profile and the border patterns have been cut—in traditional fashion—from black paper.

INSTRUCTIONS

Silhouettes are as easy to make as they were two hundred years ago. Have your model sit on a chair placed parallel to a smooth, light-colored wall, with the wall to one side of her and a light source (a bright lamp will do) to her other. The light will cast a shadow of the model's head against the wall. Trace the shadow by holding a sheet of white paper against the wall. Transfer the pattern outline to black cutting paper and cut it out. (For instructions on border cutting, see page 98.)

TIP:

- If you prefer, you can cut from white paper and apply black ink to the finished cutting.

THREE-DIMENSIONAL ROOM ORNAMENTS

Paper ornaments are often cut in Germany and Denmark. They can add both nostalgia and whimsy to Christmas trees, of course, but don't limit your use of them to Yuletide growth. They're equally eye-catching as year-long decorations. Hang one from a houseplant. Suspend another near an open window where it can swing in any gentle breeze. Decorate a shelf by tacking one or two ornaments to its edge or suspend a decorative cutting from a lamp or ceiling fixture. Simple ornaments, with an uncut area on which to write, make unique gift tags too.

INSTRUCTIONS

Follow the directions for the Christmas Tree Ornaments on pages 81 and 82. These three-dimensional cuttings are assembled in exactly the same way.

TIPS:

■ By all means, cut from colored paper if you like, but do shop for a fade-free variety. Ornaments that sway in sunlight are especially susceptible to fading.

■ Assemble three or four of these ornaments and hang them as a mobile.

Three Dimensional Room Ornaments
© Marie-Helene Grabman

STENCILS

Stenciling is the art of applying color through patterns cut out of an impervious material. Its greatest advantage is that it allows the artist to create repetitive designs from a single, cut pattern. Stencil patterns—for centuries made from paper—have been used throughout the world to paint walls, fabrics, furniture, and floors. If you enjoy the simple project presented here, which will introduce you only to the most basic elements of stenciling, by all means pursue your interest further. There are many informative books available to help you along the way.

INSTRUCTIONS

The elements of stencil cutting are much the same as those for cutting paper; in fact, the greatest difference lies in the materials used. Because ordinary papers absorb moisture and will quickly become soggy when your laden paintbrush touches them, you'll need to purchase some stencil paper. This is semi-transparent and has been coated to prevent moisture absorption. Clear acetate is a good alternative. You'll also need some stencil brushes. These are thick and bushy;

they're used to "pounce" or dab rather than stroke the paint. Purchase acrylic paints.

Transfer the pattern to the stencil paper or acetate. Cut it out with a craft knife, but don't try to fold acetate; it will crack.

Once the stencil has been cut, prepare the surface to be painted. This project was designed for a bristol board surface, but if you choose to use it as a border pattern on a plaster wall, you will need to clean, sand, and seal the wall first.

If you're going to paint the pattern more than once (as you would if you were painting a border), measure the length of the cut portion and mark your wall accordingly, so that you will know where to place the pattern each time you move it to a new position.

Tape the pattern in place. Paint each cut section, working from its edges toward its center. If you work toward the edges, paint is likely to be brushed under the stencil and will blur the design. Wait until the paint has dried somewhat

before lifting the pattern and moving it to its next position. Wet paint will creep under the stencil if you try to move the stencil too soon. Wipe the stencil clean, tape it in place again, and repeat the painting process.

TIPS:

■ Almost any surface can be stencilled; just be sure you select the most appropriate paint for the job.

■ For special effects, apply your paint with sponges, fabrics, paint-pads, or rollers.

 DOILIES

Adaptable paper doilies are elegant additions to any table or shelf. They can be slipped under dishes, bowls, boxes, tins, and candlesticks and can even be framed. Design your own patterns—ones that will match your china, your wallpaper, or your glassware. Once you've cut two or three, you'll realize how easy it is to come up with designs that look wonderfully complex but which are really quite simple.

German bakers sometimes decorate cakes by sprinkling powdered sugar through cut paper doilies called *kuchenschnitte*. Some bakeries even have a "house" pattern, one which serves to make each lusciously sugared confection a form of portable advertising! (The largest pattern pictured here is suitable for this use.)

INSTRUCTIONS

All of the smaller patterns are cut from triple-folded paper. The kuchenschnitte (the largest pattern), though it can be cut on triple-folded paper, is easier to cut as a double fold. Enlarge and transfer it to a piece of double-folded paper that is 9" (22.9 cm) square.

Note the uncut margin around the folded edges. Cut the outer, scalloped edges first. Cut from right to left if you're right-handed and from left to right if you're left-handed, turning the paper as you cut and

keeping the scissors stationary. Next cut the inside ovals in the tulips and then the areas between the leaves. End with the teardrop shapes at the paper's folded point. Unfold and press flat.

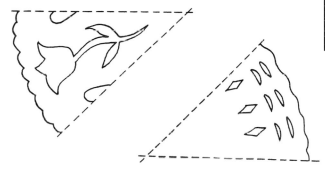

TIPS:

- Kuchenschnitte will stick to frosted cakes! Use them on unfrosted cakes only.
- Cut a slightly larger version of the kuchenschnitte to slip under the cake as a matching doily. Then wrap the cake with a horizontally folded cutting based on a similar pattern. Top it off with a three-dimensional ornament and a cut paper gift tag—and present it to someone special.
- Believe it or not, it's entirely possible to cut a round or rectangular paper tablecloth using similar designs and folding techniques. All you need is a sheet of paper that's large enough to cover your table—and patience. Tape the edges of your folded paper together with any tape that won't tear the paper once it's removed. Lay the folded paper on a hard surface (a clean floor will do) as you sketch and cut your design.

Kuchenschitte doily *(see front cover)*
Sharon Schaich

105 ◈

SHELF
LINERS

Pennsylvania German housewives of the nineteenth century proved conclusively that art can walk hand-in-hand with tidiness and frugality. When pocket money and materials were scarce, women used decoratively cut newspapers to keep the surfaces of their kitchen and pantry shelves clean, just as their German ancestors had done. Each shelf was lined with paper cut large enough so that it would drape over the edge of the shelf by a few inches. Cheerful designs were cut on the overlapping portion. Functional, disposable, inexpensive, and easy to make, these shelf liners are also a great way to practice your design and cutting skills.

INSTRUCTIONS

The patterns pictured were designed to be cut on horizontally folded, 11" (27.9 cm) x 17" (43.2 cm) paper. There's no reason you can't adapt these designs for any paper, however. Measure the length and width of the shelf you wish to

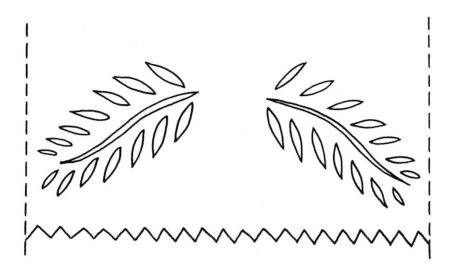

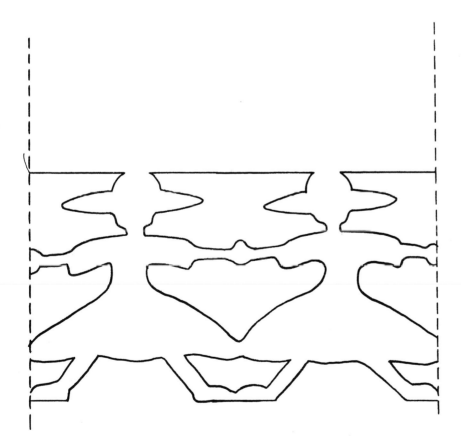

line. Add a few inches to the width. These extra inches will be the portion of your paper that you actually cut. Cut a large piece of paper to these dimensions. Fold your paper horizontally. Enlarge or reduce the pattern as necessary and transfer it to the bottom edge of your paper. Cut and unfold. Spread the uncut portion on your shelf and let the cut border hang over the edge.

TIPS:

- To cover an entire shelf, just make several cuttings and tape them together.
- Use colored paper to match the room's decor or mount the cut portion of your paper onto a long strip of colored paper.
- Be careful not to make the cut portion so long that you have trouble reaching into the shelf below!
- You don't have to line your shelves; just cut the border pattern on a narrow strip and tape or glue it to the edge of the shelf.

MOBILE

In today's busy world, it isn't often that we take time to relax—to stare into space, dream private dreams, and let ourselves unwind. Mobiles can help. Try watching one as its sways gently above your bed or favorite armchair. Its enchanting movements will enthrall you in no time at all, and within a few minutes, you'll notice your day's tensions draining slowly away.

This mobile pattern makes use of the traditional scherenschnitte heart motif and pleasant, muted colors.

INSTRUCTIONS

Select four, complementary colors of paper and decide in which order you'd like them to appear in your mobile; the largest pattern will hang at the bottom. Starting with Pattern 1, fold a 6" (15.2 cm) x 8" (20.3 cm) piece of paper in half so that it becomes 6" (15.2 cm) x 4" (10.2 cm). Transfer Pattern 1 to the paper's surface.

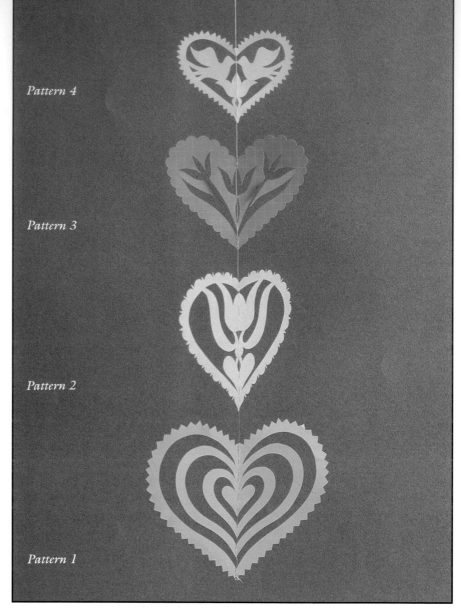

Mobile
© 1992, Sharon Schaich

Begin cutting from the outside edge of the heart. Next, starting from the folded edge, cut the smaller enclosed areas. Then cut out the larger enclosed areas. Work from right to left if you're right-handed and left to right if you're left-handed. Turn the paper as you cut, and keep the scissors stationary.

Press the finished cutting to flatten it. Follow the same steps to complete Patterns 2, 3, and 4.

Thread a needle and knot the thread's end. String the pressed hearts together by basting through the center of each heart, working

from the largest to the smallest heart. Take tiny stitches and remember to backstitch at the top and bottom of each heart in order to prevent the hearts from slipping on the thread. When you reach the top of the smallest heart, make a loop with the remaining thread.

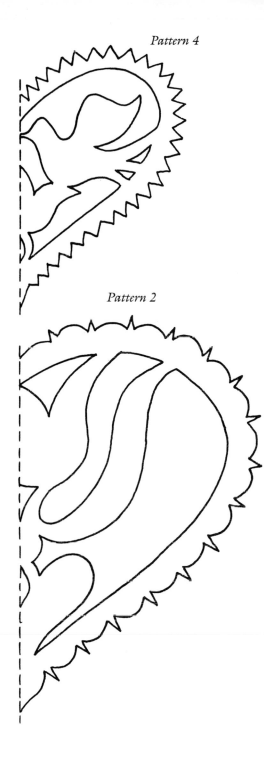

Pattern 4

Pattern 2

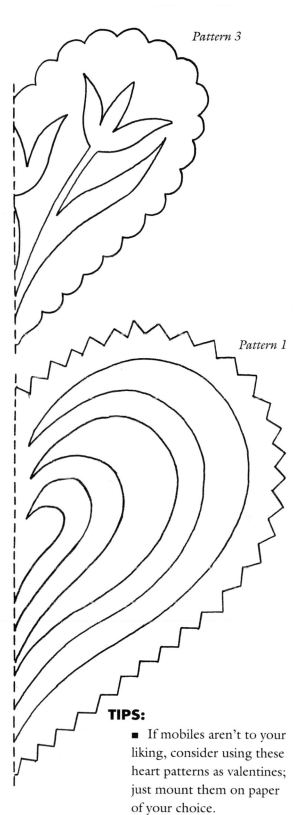

Pattern 3

Pattern 1

TIPS:

■ If mobiles aren't to your liking, consider using these heart patterns as valentines; just mount them on paper of your choice.

■ For a more elaborate mobile, suspend multiple heart cuttings from thin wooden dowels.

FOR ITS OWN SAKE:

ART &
WHIMSY

When a wall in your home needs decoration, don't rummage through the closet for an old print or bother to commission an oil portrait. Take out those scissors and create something you know you'll like. Almost any pattern, including those provided in the previous sections of this book, can be adapted for framing. What better way to brighten the interior of your home than to hang your own cut work.

 BIRD ON
A BRANCH

The delicate, perched bird featured here didn't take hours to cut. The pattern—based on an early American motif—is relatively easy to follow, yet the finished piece would look well in almost any setting.

INSTRUCTIONS

Sandwich your fragile cutting paper between the pattern and another piece of paper. Then cut through all three layers at once. Staple the sheets together before you start, so that the tissue doesn't slip. The outer paper layers serve to protect the cutting paper between them from unsightly tears.

To mount tissue, start by gluing the center of the cutting only. Working out toward the edges, apply very small amounts of glue to a few spots on the cutting's back and press them in place. Work slowly. When you've aligned and glued one area, move on to the next. Use a ruler to align the borders.

TIPS:

■ Remember to reverse the pattern when you transfer it or this asymmetrical bird will end up looking in the opposite direction when you've finished cutting it.

■ Leave a few of the interior sections unglued. The shadows cast by sections that stand away from the mounting will add an interesting three-dimensional quality to the finished piece.

YOUNG MAN'S PERSPECTIVE

It's tempting (but wrong) to think of papercutting as an exclusively female pastime. Some of the oldest extant cuttings were crafted by men, and there are many men who participate in this art form today. The double-folded pattern pictured here was designed and cut free-hand by a fourteen-year-old boy who had no formal training as a papercutter.

INSTRUCTIONS

These patterns are cut on triple-folded paper. Just transfer and cut.

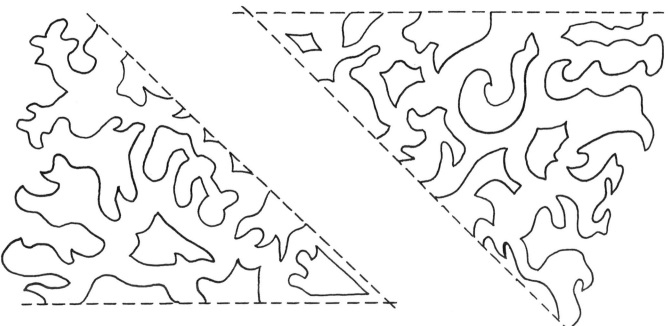

DANCING TRIBAL WOMEN

Native American people believe that there are five tribes of *two-leggeds*: Black, Brown, Red, White, and Yellow. The figures in this layered project represent those tribes and the dance with which they celebrate the art of living.

The artist who designed this piece bases her technique on the Japanese cut paper art of *kiri-e* (full color appliqué). She also makes her own paper by harvesting, processing, and dyeing leaves and vines of the kudzu plant. If kudzu isn't one of your backyard favorites, and your papermaking skills are non-existent, just purchase handmade paper instead.

INSTRUCTIONS

No pattern is provided for this project as the actual figures are easily drawn. Remember as you work that handmade paper sometimes has a rough and a smooth side; your finished project should display the interesting textures on the rough side.

You will be cutting a total of thirteen pieces: five faces, five dresses, one outline of a row of figures (with long strips extending from the first and last arms), a sky, and an earth. Select thin handmade paper or you won't be able to cut through the folded layers. Before you start, choose paper colors for each piece.

Start with the piece of paper from which your figure outline will be cut. Fold it—smooth side up—four times (accordion-style) to create five sections, but make the first and last folded sections much wider than the three in the middle. (See illustration.) These two layers should extend beyond the other three. Draw the outline of a woman's figure on the uppermost folded surface, making sure that the figure itself does not extend onto the additional length of the folded sections. Also make sure that the arms are drawn so that they will link at the fold line.

Then draw a long, thin strip on the extra length of the uppermost surface, connecting it to the figure's sleeve. When you cut through the folds, the first and last figures in

your row of dancing women will have long strips attached to their outermost sleeves. These will cover the boundary between the earth and the sky. Also draw and cut the interior holes for the face and dress.

With the smooth side of the cut outline facing you, place the row of figures on a plain piece of paper and trace the interior faces and dresses. (To keep track of colors and positions, label each traced face and dress with its intended color and with the number of the figure to which it belongs.) Enlarge the traced patterns slightly so that the cut faces and dresses will be larger than the holes they are meant to cover.

Next cut these face and dress patterns out and lay them on the smooth sides of the colored papers you have chosen. Trace their shapes onto the colored papers and cut these out. Lay the colored face and dress shapes, smooth side up, above their appropriate holes on the smooth side of the row of figures. One by one, check to make certain that each cut face and dress is large enough to completely cover the face and dress holes in the row of figures.

Then spread a small amount of white glue on your finger and smear it around the circumference of the holes in the first figure. Press the cut, colored face and dress into place over the holes. Repeat this with all cut faces and dresses.

Now spread the paper you have chosen for the sky above the paper you've selected for the earth, rough side up, so that the earth overlaps the sky by 1/2" (1.3 cm). Spread the cut figures across these two pieces, checking to make sure that the figures' arms (and the two long pieces of paper at either end of the row) cover the visible line where the earth and sky meet. Rearrange the earth and sky as necessary.

Remove the figures and glue the earth and sky together. Finally, glue the row of figures to the background by applying glue to the smooth side of each figure's outline. Make sure to cover the boundary between earth and sky with the figures' arms.

TIPS:

■ If you make a mistake and end up with gaps, just glue a small piece of paper over the hole. The texture of handmade paper helps to disguise patches.
■ Frame with or without glass.
■ Spray the surface of the cutting with clear acrylic spray to protect the paper from discoloration and mold.
■ Make cards by gluing a no-fold, layered paper figure to blank, cream-colored card stock.

# CHINESE BIRDS

These brightly painted birds are typical of contemporary Chinese papercuttings, which are rarely cut on a fold. Instead, the artist stacks many sheets of thin paper in a wooden frame and a single design is carved through them all with extremely sharp knives and chisels. This technique requires years of practice. You'll probably be much happier with your finished work if you cut just one at a time!

When a batch of these cuttings is finished, sheets of tissue are placed between each one to keep them separated. The cuttings are often grouped in sets of four, six, or eight figures related to a single theme. The pattern pictured here is one of a set of eight cuttings, each of which is slightly different. Cuttings are often embellished with calligraphic ink or watercolors.

INSTRUCTIONS

If rice paper is available in your area, you may want to try it, but parchment will work just as well. Use a craft knife for all of the interior cuts. Paint your cutting either before or after it's finished. A blurred effect can be created by applying one color on top of another damp color. This technique will work well with the blended colors on flowers and leaves, but when you don't want colors to mix (between the brown stems and leaves, for instance), be sure to let one color dry before you apply the next.

TIPS:

■ Change craft knife blades frequently to avoid rough edges.

■ Remove cut slivers by stabbing them gently with your knife and lifting them out. If the cut area seems to stick to surrounding paper, cut over the original lines until it separates easily.

 ## TREE IN
BASKET

Tree-of-life motifs, like the one
featured in this traditional, single-
folded cutting, are common to both
scherenschnitte and wycinanki. Ripe
with the promise of nature's boun-
ty, these symbolic trees often
include birds or other wildlife
perched in their branches.

INSTRUCTIONS

As you cut this fairly complex, single-folded pattern, leave the interior
and exterior edges of the outer border until the very end. If you cut
the border first, it may tear while
you work on the interior.

TIP:

■ Note how well this plain
black cutting looks against its
white mat board.

Enlarge pattern 135 % to match original size.

 CAT

Animals figure prominently in papercut designs, perhaps because they offer so many possible perspectives to the cutting artist. With no more than a few strategically placed cut lines, this artist has captured the essence of a cat in waiting. The raised tail, the back leg poised for a possible jump, the chin lifted—every detail tells us that this feline sees something just out of its reach, something it wants—badly!

INSTRUCTIONS

Make a copy of the pattern (it's been reversed for you already) and fasten it to your cutting paper with tape or staples. Cut through both layers of paper at the same time. Doing this will prevent the hairline cuts in the tail and interior from tearing as you make them.

TIP:

■ If you use a craft knife and mat board, be sure that the board is relatively free of cut marks so that your knife blade won't catch on any indentations.

PROFILE

Cut paper portraiture was especially popular during the eighteenth century, when Dutch and German artists created cut designs so intricate that they looked as if they'd been drawn. Portraits needn't be quite so complex, however. This contemporary pattern was created by a young man who had never cut paper before.

INSTRUCTIONS

Cutting this pattern couldn't be easier. Just reverse the pattern, transfer it to a flat sheet of paper, and cut!

TIP:

■ If you're new to cutting (or sketching) portraits, the easiest way to design your own patterns is to start with a photograph of your subject. Study it closely. Look for the defining characteristics. In this profile cutting, for instance, the artist was impressed by the subject's locks of hair, by the lines around his eyes, and by the shadow lines on the face itself. Sketch the lines that strike you as most distinctive. Make them as wide or narrow, long or short as an actual cut might be. Start with the most noticeable lines and then add to them.

CHILDREN'S CUT WORK

Children won't need much prompting to try their hands at papercutting, and they won't require patterns either. All you'll need to do is explain how folding works, provide the paper, and pass out the blunt-tipped scissors. Let your children exercise their own creativity. Who knows? You may be helping to develop the next generation of fine papercutters!

on't feel badly if you find it difficult to dream up new subjects, styles, and techniques. Every artist needs inspiration once in awhile, and papercutters are no exception. Next time your imagination doesn't snap to attention with its familiar speed, just send it on a tour through this collection of outstanding cuttings. Designed by some of today's best papercutters—as well as some of yesterday's—these magnificently executed papercuttings are bound to supply you with new perspectives and new goals.

Let these creations incite you to action, by all means, but avoid copying them. Your imagination won't get any exercise if you do. When you see something you like—whether it's a particular folding pattern, a new way to mount a cutting, a painting technique, or unusual content—translate what you see into something uniquely your own.

CLOCKWISE FROM TOP LEFT, OPPOSITE PAGE

Star, © 1991, *Elżbieta Kaleta*

Untitled, *Nancy Tucker*

Paper Lace, *13-1/4" (33.6 cm) x 10-1/2" (26.7 cm), © 1983, Marie-Helene Grabman*

Ramesses the Great, *15-1/2" (39.4 cm) x 19" (48.3 cm), © 1983, Marie-Helene Grabman*

CLOCKWISE FROM TOP LEFT

Untitled, *Wietske Meppelink, (twelve years old)*

Esa Einay, *19" (48.3 cm) x 20" (50.8 cm), © 1990, Dan Howarth*

Heart of My Heart, *16" (40.6 cm) x 18" (45.7 cm), © 1992, Sharon Schaich*

Wash Day, *4" (10.2 cm) x 10" (25.4 cm), © 1987, Sandra Gilpin*

CONTRIBUTING
DESIGNERS

NANCY BASKET (pages 113-115) is an accomplished papermaker—and cutter—whose art reflects her Native American heritage. She has been Chairman of the Education Committee of the South Carolina Crafts Center, has resident artist status in both North and South Carolina, and has taught papermaking in the South Carolina public schools. Nancy operates her own business, Kudzu Kabin Designs, in Jonesville, South Carolina.

DEBORAH CARTER (pages 70-71, 81-84, 88-89 borders, 99 photo border, 100 border, 118), who lives in Brevard, North Carolina, is married to an Episcopal priest and has three sons. She attended a series of classes taught by Elzbieta Kaleta (see below) and has been designing, cutting, and selling wycinanki and scherenschnitte for two years. Her fourteen-year-old son, Caleb (page 112), learned to cut paper by watching his mother.

CHARLIE COVINGTON (pages 72, 75, 99 fern pattern, 120), a college student majoring in Environmental Studies, had never made a papercutting before he created some for this book. Charlie lives in Asheville, North Carolina.

ALEX FONG (pages 6, 29, 44, 67, 128), whose award-winning cut work has been displayed in fine art shows across the United States, resides in Oak Ridge, Tennessee. He was trained to his craft by his grandfather in Shanghai and has been cutting paper since he was five years old. Alex has taught papercutting to both children and adults.

SANDRA GILPIN (pages 19, 48-51, 124, 127), who resides in Hanover, Pennsylvania, is a professional papercutter, a juried member of the Pennsylvania Guild of Craftsmen, and a founding member of the Guild of American Papercutters. Her work, which reflects her Lancaster County, Pennsylvania heritage, has been featured in national publications and displayed in private collections. Her commissioned pieces include one made for Willard Scott of "The Today Show."

MARIE-HELENE GRABMAN (Cover inset—© 1992, pages 6, 15, 54-55, 62, 65, 66, 101, 122, 123, 126), whose uniquely detailed work combines secular and religious influences, as well as American and European styles, was introduced to scherenschnitte by her grand-mother. She displays her work in juried shows and has won several awards. A resident of Charlotte, North Carolina, Ms. Grabman is a member of the Guild of American Papercutters and of the Piedmont Craftsmen, Inc.

ELŻBIETA KALETA (pages 6, 19, 21, 25, 38, 53, 56-61, 63-64, 122), who was born in Krakow, Poland, has lived in Albuquerque, New Mexico since 1984. Her wycinanki—some deeply rooted in her own Polish heritage and others rendered in what Elżbieta calls her Southwest style—have been exhibited internationally. Elżbieta is a member of the Guild of American Papercutters and of the Artist's Advocacy Committee of the Santa Fe Council for the Arts. She is also a recipient of a Folk Art Grant from New Mexico State, Arts Division and has participated in numerous juried art shows and invitational demonstrations.

Eighteen year-old *JOHN MYRES* (page 76 small standing tags, pages 96-97) has already won an award for his design work. He lives in Asheville, North Carolina, and hopes to become a commercial artist.

SHARON FARQUHAR SCHAICH (Doily on cover, 39, and 105; pages 41, 108-109, 124) helped to found the Guild of American Papercutters in 1988 and is its Director-at-Large. She is a state juried member of the Pennsylvania Guild of Craftsmen and Director-at-Large of its State Board. Mrs. Schaich has been juried into Early American Life's *Directory of American Craftsmen* for the past three years. A native of Ohio, she now lives with her family in Lititz, Pennsylvania. Mrs. Schaich's intricate cuttings reflect her interest in working with colored papers and applied watercolors.

ALISON COSGROVE TANNER and her mother *GLORIA COSGROVE* (pages 78-80, 85-87) date their mutual fascination with papercutting back to 1966. This mother-daughter team has written a book on the craft and operates a mail-order business (Papercuttings by Alison, 404 Partridge Circle, Sarasota, FL 34236) as well.

NANCY TUCKER (page 76 angels, pages 85-87 house-and-trees card, pages 90-91, 94-95, 98, 122) has been a papercutter for over ten years and has a strong interest in traditional Pennsylvania German scherenschnitte. She has sold her work in Oklahoma and in Asheville, North Carolina, where she and her daughter now reside.

Love Me Knot

Love Me Knot
6-1/2" (16.5 cm) x 14" (35.6 cm)
© 1983, *Marie-Helene Grabman*

CONTRIBUTING DESIGNERS

And thanks to...

ROBERTA BATES (page 88), whose calligraphy embellishes the birth announcement.

JESSIE BROWN, AUSTIN SCONYERS-SNOW, and *CHRISTINE WOOLERY* (page 121) for their creative contributions.

TAMAR FISHMAN (pages 5 and 14), who graciously submitted her stunning cut work for reproduction.

SANDRA GILPIN, for her advice on painting and for her research materials.

MARIE-HELENE GRABMAN, for having shared invaluable historical information.

CATHERINE GROSFILS, Audiovisual Editorial Librarian at the Colonial Williamsburg Foundation, whose help in locating the valentine pictured on page 18 was deeply appreciated.

DAN HOWARTH (pages 15, 124), whose cuttings reflect both his faith and his remarkable skills—and to his wife, *DEBBY*, who beat our deadline! Dan and Debby reside in Baltimore, Maryland.

TAMMY MCNABB, who "tested" some patterns, embellished others, and made every effort to keep the author sane.

LOTTIE SCONYERS (pages 10, 116, and 117), for the loan of her Chinese cut work.

CHARLOTTE SMITH, for her fluent translations and infinite patience.

UITGEVERIJ CANTECLEER BV (publishers), de Bilt, Holland, for permission to reproduce photographs from *Leer Knippende Zien* by I.G. Kerp-Schlesinger, 1970. (Pages 3, 8, 11, 12, 13, 16 silhouettes, 17, 45, 124)

Photographs on pages 22, 23, 26, 27, 30, 31, 33-37, 39, 40, 44, 46-48, 51, 54, 58, 59, 62, 63, 65-70, 72-76, 79, 81, 83, 85, 88, 90, 93, 95, 97-102, 104-106, 108, 110, 112, 113, 116, 118, 119, 121 were taken by *EVAN BRACKEN*, Light Reflections, Hendersonville, North Carolina.

BIBLIOGRAPHY

ANDREW, H. E. LAYE. *The Arco Encyclopedia of Crafts.* New York: Arco Publishing Co., 1978.

BELL, LILLIAN A. *Papyrus, Tapa, Amate & Rice Paper: Papermaking in Africa, the Pacific, Latin America & Southeast Asia.* 2d ed., rev. McMinnville, Oregon: Liliaceae Press, 1985.

DRWAL, FRANCES. *Polish Wycinanki Designs.* Owings Mill, Maryland: Stemmer House Publishers, 1984.

EVERS, INGE. *Het Complete Papier Boek.* de Bilt, Holland: Cantecleer bv, 1991.

FIELD, JUNE. *Collecting Georgian and Victorian Crafts.* New York: Charles Scribner's Sons, 1973.

HOPF, CLAUDIA. *Scherenschnitte: Traditional Papercutting.* 1977. Reprint. Lebanon, Pennsylvania: Applied Arts Publishers, 1987.

JABLONSKI, RAMONA. *Folk Art Designs from Polish Wycinanki and Swiss and German Scherenschnitte.* Owings Mill, Maryland: Stemmer House Publishers, 1978.

JACKSON, MRS. E. NEVILL. *Silhouettes: A History and Dictionary of Artists.* New York: Dover Publications, 1981.

JACKSON, VALERIE. *Crafts: Yesterday's Crafts for Today.* London: Lutterworth Press, 1979.

JOHNSON, PAULINE. *Creating With Paper: Basic Forms and Variations.* New York: Dover Publications, 1986.

KERP-SCHLESINGER, I.G. *Leer Knippende Zien.* 2nd ed. de Bilt, Holland: Uitgeverij Cantecleer, 1981.

LONGENECKER, MARTHA, ed. *Paper Innovations: Handmade Paper and Handmade Objects of Cut, Folded and Molded Paper.* Seattle, Washington: University of Washington Press, 1986.

MELCHERS, BERND, ed. *Traditional Chinese Cut-Paper Designs.* New York: Dover Publications, 1978.

MENTEN, THEODORE, selected by. *Chinese Cut-Paper Designs.* New York: Dover Publications, 1975.

NAKANO, EISHA WITH BARBARA B. STEPHAN. *Japanese Stencil Dyeing: Paste-Resist Techniques.* New York: John Weatherhill, 1982.

NEWMAN, THELMA R., JAY HARTLEY NEWMAN, AND LEE SCOTT NEWMAN. *Paper as Art and Craft: The Complete Book of the History and Processes of the Paper Arts.* New York: Crown Publishers, 1973.

The Living Tree
16" (40.6 cm) x 22-1/2" (57.2 cm)
© 1986, Sandra Gilpin

ROBACKER, EARL F. "Cutting Up for Fancy." *Pennsylvania Folklife* 10 (Fall 1959) : 2-10.

SHANNON, FAITH. *Paper Pleasures: The Creative Guide to Papercraft.* New York: Grove Weidenfeld (In association with Il Papiro), 1987.

SPERO, JAMES, ed. *Japanese Floral Stencil Designs.* New York: Dover Publications, 1991.

TEMKO, FLORENCE. *Chinese Paper Cuts.* San Francisco: China Books and Periodicals, 1982.

TREINEN, SARA JANE AND NANCY REAMES, eds. *Better Homes and Gardens Paper Crafts.* Meredith Corporation: Des Moines, Iowa, 1989.

INDEX

Peacock
11" (27.9 cm) x 14" (35.6 cm)
Alex Fong